Momma n 'Em Said

Said

The Treasury of Southern Sayings

By Tim Heaton and generations of Southerners

DEDICATIONS

To my parents, Tim and Gayle Heaton, who embraced Southern culture and instilled a love of the South to their family. One of their favorite sayings is: "This food is hardly fit to eat." Meaning – it's delicious!

Ed Meek, who inspired generations of writers and journalists at the University of Mississippi. Ed is particularly fond of: "Close that door, you weren't born in a barn!"

And to my wife Linda, who's editing and support made this book possible. Linda's favorite is: "Raising kids is like being pecked to death by a chicken."

CONTENTS

Book One: the Best of Southern Sayings
Verse One: Greetings

Verse Two: Let's Chew the Fat

Verse Three: More Personalities

Verse Four: Are You Well? It's a Deep Subject!

Verse Five: The Wisdom of Ages·

Verse Six: Momma Also Said, "A Word to the Wise is Sufficient·"

Book Three: A Sample of Uniquely Southern Terms.

Book Four: Contributors and Their Favorite Sayings.

ABOUT THIS BOOK

My original purpose for writing this book was to preserve as many Southern sayings as possible. There may well come a day when these gems of wisdom and heartfelt expressions are simply forgotten due to the media's incessant drone of generic offerings.

As I asked folks for their favorite sayings, I soon recognized that I had hit a cord with people that grew up in the South, or those who from good fortune had come to be Southerners. I fit the latter case: I was born in the north, but grew up in Mississippi. Just as immigrants to America once had, my family completely immersed themselves in the local culture and over time - became Southerners. Today, I often describe myself as a "wanna-be Southerner", which more often than not, puzzles folks in the north. I console myself with the fact that one never hears of a Southerner claiming to be a New Englander, Mid-Westerner or other some-such. The Southern ethos seeps slowly and permanently into one's soul - like oil into stone.

As you read through this book, I hope you too will find yourself carried back in time. If I "did this book proud" as my parents would say, you will find yourself crying and laughing all at once.

How to Enjoy this Book

Each saying is assigned to one of sixty-two categories so that you may find the appropriate saying for any occasion. There are almost 2,000 Southern sayings and terms from over 400 contributors which are collected into four books. Many of the sayings are commonly heard. If a contribution was unusual, I recognized the contributor.

Book One is the "best of" Southern sayings. Each phrase has a category in a verse. There are eight verses: Verse One-Greetings, Verse Two-Let's Chew the Fat, Verse Three-More Personalities, Verse Four-Are You Well? It's a Deep Subject!, Verse Five-The Wisdom of Ages, Verse Six-Momma Also Said, "A Word to the Wise is Sufficient.", Verse Seven- I'm Glad You Asked!, and Verse Eight-Goodbye. The verses are arranged in a sequential order that one might observe in any social setting. That is, it starts out with greetings, and then goes on to: weather, food, gossip, some of momma n 'ems often ignored advice, and finally - goodbye.

Book Two is a categorized list of all 1,600 Southern sayings that I collected. There are 62 categories: Argumentative, Bellyaching, Blue, Busy, Capable, Charming, Chatty, Confused, Courtship, Dearly Departed, Dimwits, Dirt Poor, Effortless, Elders, Exclamations, Excuse Me, Glad, Goodbye, Gossip, Greetings, Health, Homely, How Much?, Hungry, Insults, Intoxicated, Lazy, Luck-Both Kinds, Momma Said, Nervous, No, Odors, Plumpish, Proverbs, Saints, Scolding, Scrawny, Shiftless, Skinflint, Speed-Fast, Speed-Slow, Stubborn,

Surprised, Temperature, Testy, Threats, Time, Touched, Tough, Trifling, Troublesome, Villains, Vittles, Weary, Well-healed, Weather, Yes, and Yonder.

Book Three is a list of terms that are unique to the South, although the list could be far greater, these terms were ones I ran across while compiling all the sayings. They are included because I thought you might enjoy them.

Book Four acknowledges the 420 contributors to the book and contains a sample of their contributions. If this book touches you, you have these folks to thank.

Book One

Verse One: Greetings

How's ur Momma n' Em?
Gimme a yankee dime!

I haven't seen you in a minute!

You're a sight for sore eyes!

Doing Good
Fair to Middlin'.

Better than snuff and ain't half as dusty.

"Still kickin' but not high, still floppin' but can't fly.*Audrey Wright

Fine as a frog's hair split up the middle and tied at both ends.

I'm all wool and a yard wide.

If I knew you was coming, I'd have baked a cake!

If I was any happier I'd be twins.

Yes (with style!)

Might as well. Can't dance, never could sing, and it's too wet to plow.

Darn tootin'!

Does a fat baby fart?

Does a one legged duck swim in a circle?

Good Lord willing and the creek don't rise.

I could sit still for that.

Is a frog's ass watertight?

Sure as a cat's got climbing gear.

No (Hell No!)

Hard sayin' not knowin'.

I'd rather sandpaper a bobcat's ass in a phone booth. *Derek Brewer

Like a kerosene cat in Hell with gasoline drawers on. (No chance)

That will go over like a pregnant pole-vaulter.

That's a gracious plenty.

When my coon gets fat.

You might as well shove your money up a wolf's ass and
watch him run over the hill.

Where? It's Just Over Yonder.
A piece down the road.

I had to grease the wagon twice before hit the main road.

Just a hop skip and a jump.   *Judy Noble

Over yonder in the edge of nothin'.

They live so far out they have to pipe in sunshine.

Hungry?
I am so hungry I can see biscuits walking on crutches! *Janice
Box-Franklin

I could eat the north end of a south-bound goat.

I'd eat the balls off a low flying duck!

I'm so hungry I could eat a frozen dog!

I'm so hungry I'm fartin' cobwebs.

My belly thinks my throat's been cut.

Vittles

Anything with a beak and a wing is a beautiful thing.
*Cammie Beckwith Bennett

That is cooked to a turn!

So good I could slap granny!

I've seen animals hurt worse than that get well. (Too rare meat)

It was so good it would have brought tears to a glass eye.

It'll make your liver quiver and your bladder splatter.

I hope I remembered my space panties.

So bad it would snatch the taste right out of her mouth.

This coffee is so strong it'll walk into your cup.

This will make your tongue slap your brains out.

Verse Two: Let's Chew the Fat

Gossip

Everything she's got is out on the showroom floor.

Her hair looks like it caught on fire and somebody put it out with a brick.

Her jeans are so tight, you can see Washington grinning on the quarter in her pocket.

His pants were so tight that if he farted, he'd blow his boots off.

He was so deep in jail he'll have to be fed beans with a sling-shot!

I wouldn't pee in her ear if her brain was on fire.

If she had one more wrinkle, she could screw her hat on.

Just wear beige and keep quiet.

In those jeans she looks like two Buicks fighting for a parking place.

Momma's baby - Daddy's maybe.

She wouldn't go to a funeral unless it was theirs.

She's a caution.

She's been "storked".

They are as welcome as an outhouse breeze.

They ate supper before they said grace.

Weather

Cold as a cast iron commode.

Cold enough to freeze the balls off a pool table.

It's coming up a bad cloud.

Devil's beatin' his wife with a frying pan.

Hotter than a four-peckered billy goat.

Hotter than a popcorn fart.

Hotter'n seven Hells.

It's gonna be a frog-strangler.

Raining so hard the animals are starting to pair up.

So cold we got dogs stuck to fire hydrants all over town.

So dry the trees are whistling for the dogs.

So foggy, the birds are walking.

Courtship

That man has got a thumping gizzard for a heart.

I've got church in the morning. (You better hurry!)

If I had that swing on my back porch I'd ride it every night.

If it has tires or testicles it's gonna give you trouble.

If promises were persimmons, possums could eat good at her place.

If you can sleep with 'em, I can eat with 'em!

Like putting gas in a car that you've already wrecked.

Her back side looks like two Indian boys fighting under a blanket.

She got her trotting harness on.

She was batting her eyes like a toad in a hail storm.

Well, ain't he just the tom-cat's kitten?

You can't ride two horses with one ass.

Verse Three: More Personalities

Argumentative
He would argue with a stop sign!

She could start an argument in an empty house.

Bellyaching
If a bullfrog had wings, he wouldn't bump his ass when he jumped.

If your aunt had nuts she'd be your uncle.

Wish in one hand and shit in the other and see which one fills up first.

Capable
He could talk the dogs off a meat truck.

If she says her hen dips snuff, you can look under the wing for a can.

Smart as a tree full of owls.

Charming

Cute as a bug's ear.

Cuter than pig nipples.

Pretty as a mess of fried catfish.

She's pretty as a speckled pup.

She's finer than frog hair split eight ways!

Chatty

He blew in on his own wind.

He shoots off his mouth so much he must eat bullets for breakfast.

He'd drive a wooden Indian crazy.

Her mouth runs like a boarding house toilet.

They were vaccinated with a Victrola.

Windy as a sack full of farts.

Shiftless

Handy as a cow on crutches.

He's about as useful as a pogo stick in quicksand.

I need him like a tomcat needs a trousseau.

Useless as teats on a lightbulb.

Worthless as a sidesaddle on a sow.

Homely

About as sexy as socks on a billy goat.

Born short and slapped flat.

Has to sneak up on a water fountain to get a drink.

He looks like something the dog's been keeping under the porch.

He must have been inside the outhouse when lightning struck.

He must have stuck his finger in a light socket while his mama was beating him with an ugly stick.

His momma borrows another baby for church.

I wonder what she would charge to haunt a house?

She had a face so ugly she wore out two bodies.

She's ugly enough to stop an eight-day clock.

So ugly she'd make a freight train take a dirt road.

That face might not stop a clock but it'd sure raise Hell with watches.

Uglier than a lard bucket full of armpits.

Plumpish

Fatter than the town dog. *Whitney Crow Smith

He didn't get a round mouth by eating square meals.

It takes two dogs to bark at her.

Piggy Wiggly hires a rodeo clown to distract her when grocery shopping.

Dirt Poor

Don't have a pot to piss in or a window to throw it out of.

I couldn't buy a hummingbird on a string for a nickel.

We were so poor growing up, my brothers had to ride double on a stick horse.

Too poor to paint, too proud to whitewash.

We were so poor we had to use a possum as a yard dog.

Lazy

Born in the middle of the week and looking both ways for Sunday.

He follows the shade around the house.

He wouldn't take time to say "shit" if he had a mouthful of it.

He's so lazy he calls the dog inside to see if it's raining.

Luck, Both Kinds

Good Luck says, "Open your mouth and shub your eyes."

I could fall into a barrel of teats and come out sucking my thumb.

He could sit on the fence and the birds would feed him.

He's riding the gravy train with biscuit wheels.

Touched

As crazy as an outhouse rat.

Crazy as a soup sandwich.

He's nuttier than a squirrel turd.

He's lost his vertical hold.

The cheese slid off of that boy's cracker!

Saints

He's so honest you could shoot craps with him over the phone.

Scrawny

A strong fart in a whirlwind would blow him away.

He swapped legs with a jaybird and got cheated out of a butt.

He'd have to stand up twice to cast a shadow.

She's a carpenter's dream: flat as a board and ain't never been nailed.

Dimwits

He's as lost as last year's Easter eggs.

His brain rattles around like a BB in a boxcar.

If brains were dynamite, she wouldn't have enough to blow her nose.

If I put his brain in a gnat's butt, it would fly backwards.

If leather were brains, he wouldn't have enough to saddle a June-bug.

Not the sharpest spoon in the drawer.

Dumber than a football bat.

Skinflints

He'd squeeze a nickel until the buffalo farts.

If he walks over a penny, his butt quivers.

She wouldn't give a nickel to see Jesus riding a bicycle.

Stubborn

Dug in like an Appalachian tick.

Like a billy goat: hard head and stinking butt.

Stubborn as a blue-nosed mule.

Tough

Could chew up nails and spit out a barbed wire fence.

Could go bear hunting with a switch.

He whips his own ass twice a week.

He's scared of nothing but spiders and dry counties.

Tougher than a one eared alley cat.

Villains

Going to blow the gates of Hell wide open when he goes.

He's lower than a snake fart.

One of them will lie and the other one will swear to it.

So crooked that if he swallowed a nail he'd spit up a corkscrew.

Too mean for Jesus and too dumb for the Devil.

Well, they deserve a front seat in Hell for that. *Andrea Jenea Bobo

Well-healed

Got enough money to burn a wet mule.

He buys a new boat when he gets the other one wet.

He's richer than ten inches up a mule's butt.

Walkin' in tall cotton since Napoleon was in knee pants.

Verse Four: Are You Well? It's a Deep Subject!

Busy

Busier than a cat burying shit on a marble floor.

Busier than a one-armed monkey with two peckers.

Busy as a cat on a hot tin roof.

I'm busier than a borrowed mule.

Confused

As lost as Hogan's goat.

Confused as a fart in a fan factory.

I didn't know whether to scratch my watch or wind my butt.

I don't know if I found my rope or lost my cow. *Holly Crim Springer

Lost as last year's Easter egg.

Tickled

Happier than a tornado in a trailer park.

Happier than two dead pigs in the sunshine.

I'm so tickled I can't get my leg down.

If I was any happier I'd be twins.

Like a dog with two tails.

Health

I feel like a bag of smashed assholes.

I feel like I got eaten by a bear and shit off a cliff.

I'm so sick I'd have to get better to die.

I feel like I was rode hard and put away wet.

Nervous

Like a frog on the freeway with a busted jumper.

Like a long tail cat in a room full of rocking chairs.

Like a porcupine in a balloon factory.

You couldn't drive a toothpick up my butt with a

sledgehammer.

Blue

Lower than a snakes belly in a wagon rut.

If momma ain't happy, ain't nobody happy.

Swinging my legs from a dime.

Surprised

Butter my butt and call me a biscuit!

Like finding a feather on a frog.

Makes a bulldog want to hug a ham. *Art Bowman

Well I'll be a sock eyed mule!

Well don't that beat a goose gobbling! *Mark Davis

Testy

About to have a dying duck fit!

It's stuck in my craw like hair on a biscuit.

Madder than a boiled owl.

Madder than a hornet in a rainstorm.

Madder than a wet settin' hen.

That dills my pickle!

Weary

I feel like 10 miles of bad road.

I was born tired and since have suffered a relapse.

One wheel down and the axle dragging.

Shot at and missed, shit at and hit.

Slightly burned out, but still smokin'.

Verse Five: The Wisdom of Ages.

Momma Said

"If you fall out of that tree and break your leg don't come running to me." *Phil Tillman

A hard head makes a soft behind.

Act like you got some raisin'.

Close the door, you're letting the flies out. (In)

Don't be ugly to your sister.

Don't get your cows running.

Don't look at me in that tone of voice. *Ann Fassetta

Go cut me a switch — and if it's not to my liking I will cut one for you.

Have clean drawers on if you're going somewhere — you may get in a car accident. *Fran Hart and Gail Bouldin

I brought you into this world I'll take you out. *Eddy Hays

I got one nerve left and you are jumping all over it.

If you can go out on Saturday night you can go to church on Sunday morning.

Is this what you wanna be doing when Jesus comes back?
*Samantha Reed

Keep it up and you're gonna be sitting at the right foot of
the Devil. *Andrea Jenea Bobo

Kids could break a second-hand anvil with a turkey feather

Make sure you wash where the Yankee shot you. (Navel)
*Lynn Poor

Me 'n you are about to have a "come to Jesus" meeting.

Pretty is as pretty does.

Quit acting like your daddy's people.

That's your red wagon to pull. *Lisa McGee

The Lord greased your butt and slid you down a rainbow.
(Answer to the.) *Kathleen Gallagher Bishop

Why, bless your little pea-pickin' heart.

You are acting like a cat's aunt Jane. *Dan Walker

You can just get glad in the same britches you got mad in.

You have something in your mouth that I wouldn't hold in
my hand. *Kathleen Gallagher Bishop

Your face is gonna freeze like that.

Your momma wasn't a glass blower· (I can't see TV·)

Proverbs

A cat can have kittens in an oven, but that don't make 'em biscuits·

A gallant retreat is better than a bad stand·

A new broom sweeps clean, but an old one knows where the dirt is·

A wink is as good as a nod to a blind horse· (Some people just can't take a hint·)

Better to keep your mouth shut and seem a fool than to open it and remove all doubt·

Don't argue with idiots, they will drag you down to their level and beat you with experience·

Don't try to rake up the family secrets of every sausage you eat·

Don't skinny dip with snapping turtles·

Fools' names and fools' faces always appear in public places·
*David Gaddie

If you can't race it or take it to bed, you don't need it·

Live and learn, die and know it all.

Make haste - there ain't no coming back. *Carolyn Slay-Jones

Never sign anything by neon.

When you find yourself in a hole - quit digging.

Verse Six: Momma Also Said, "A Word to the Wise is Sufficient."

Intoxicated

Drunker than a bicycle. *Kathy Hilliard Sanders

He was drunker than Cooter Brown on the 4th of July. (Cooter stayed drunk during the entire Civil War)

He's so drunk he couldn't hit the floor with his hat.

Tore up from the floor up.

Insults

Almost as smart as people say he thinks he is.

Can't never could.

Give me a fly-snapper and I'll help you kill it. (That hairdo is outta control.)

He's the cream of the crap, and the crap of the cream.

I've stepped over better than you looking for a place to piss.

If I want your opinion I will unscrew the top of your head and dip it out. *Fred Doane

If stupid could fly, you'd be a jet.

When you die you're gonna have to rise up to find Hell.

You are going to Hell on a scholarship.

You know I wouldn't shit you. You're my favorite turd.

You now as much about that as a hog knows about Sunday.
*Tom Owens

You shouldn't be hunting anything smarter than you.

You smell like you want to be left alone.

Your momma should have killed you and sold the milk.

Your truck couldn't pull a fat baby off a tricycle.

Scolding
I can tell you a thing or two 'bout a thing or two.

I got a bone to pick with you.

If I tell you a rooster can pull a wagon, hitch'em up.

My cow died last night, so I don't need your bull.

Who's plucking this chicken, you or me?

Threats

Don't let your bulldog mouth overload your hummingbird ass.

Don't pee down my back and tell me it's raining!

I have three speeds: on, off, and don't push your luck.

I'll kill you and swear you died.

I'll knock your teeth down your throat and you'll spit 'em out in single file.

If you don't stop, I'll tear your arm off and beat you to death with the bloody stump.

Sis on you Pister, you ain't so muckin' fuch! (We love to swap letters on curse words.)

Time to paint your butt white and run with the antelope.

You are so full of shit your eyes are brown.

You better give your heart to Jesus, because your butt is mine.

Just a Little More Diplomacy

Excuse me
I gotta go see a man about a horse.

I gotta piss like a Russian race horse at the derby getting chased by a glue truck.

I'm going to see the turtle take to water. *Kevin Spencer

The only thing we got to fear is a public toilet seat.

Exclamations!

I swannie! (Many grandmothers would not say "swear")

Cotton-picker!

Doesn't that just beat all you ever stepped in?

Good heavenly days!

Hellfire and damnation!

Hells' bells!

I do declare!

I'll dance at your wedding!

I'll be dipped in shit and rolled in cracker crumbs!

Lord help me over the fence! *Mandy Graham

My stars and garters!

Piss on that step ant! *Wade Hampton Sutherland

Shit fire and save the matches!

Well thank you Billy Sunday!

Verse Seven: I'm Glad You Asked!

How Much?

As country as cornflakes.

Common as goat nuts.

Dark as the inside of a cow.

Deaf in one ear and can't hear out of the other.

Flashy as a rat with a gold tooth.

He looked like a pig on ice.

I was stuck hub deep to a Ferris wheel.

I'm prouder of that than a hound pup is of his first flea.

If that don't tickle your fancy, I'll kiss your ass until your hat flies off. *Jeri Hale

It's quieter than a mouse pissing on cotton.

It's more than I can say grace over.

Like a popcorn fart in Hell. (Ignored)

Like a rooster in an empty hen-house. (Frustrated)

Not big enough to cuss the cat in.

Not too pretty for nice, but great for good.

That fits tighter than socks on a rooster.

You can't sling a cat without hitting one. (Common)

You're swinging that driver like a washer woman.

Odors

Gag a maggot!

He was farting like a pack mule.

It smelled worse than a dead skunk that just crawled out of another dead skunk's ass.

It smells like tomcats fighting.

That smells like the shithouse door on a shrimp boat.

That stinks so bad it could knock a buzzard off a gut wagon.

That stinks to high heaven.

That would gag a maggot on a gut wagon.

Speed - Fast

Faster than a frog shot through a barn.

Faster than a one-legged man in a butt-kicking competition.

He can blow out the lamp and jump into bed before the room gets dark.

He ran like a scalded haint.

He ran like his feet were on fire and his butt was catching.

He went through that like Sherman went through Georgia.

I am off like a dirty shirt! *Fred Doane

It happened faster than a knife fight in a phone booth.

Like a dose of salts through a widow woman.

Ran like a turpentine-ed cat.

Quick as a politician's promise.

Took off like Moody's goose.

Speed - Slow

He runs just like a candle.

Like a cat eating a grindstone.

She has two speeds. Slow and stop.

Slower than a herd of turtles stampeding through peanut

butter.

Slower than a drunk snail crawling on molasses up an ice hill in January.

Temperature

Cold as a frosted frog.

Cold as a well digger's butt.

Hot as a depot stove.

Hotter n' Hell's basement on the day of reckoning.

Hotter than a billy goat with a blowtorch.

Hotter than a three-balled tomcat.

Hotter than Satan's housecat.

It's hotter than Satan's toenails in here! *Marcy Foster

Troublesome

About as hard as trying to herd chickens.

Easy as pissing up a rope.

I'm going to see to it that it happens, even if it harelips the governor.

Like putting socks on a rooster.

Like snatching shit from a flying goose.

Like trying to catch a cat in a whirlwind.

Like trying to nail Jell-O to a tree.

Trifling

I don't have a dog in that fight

I wasn't sitting on the bedpost.

It's like two mules fighting over a turnip.

That ain't worth the powder to blow it to Hell.

Time

Ain't been home since Josie was a calf. *Mike Autry

It's time to fish or cut bait.

I got up at the butt-crack of dawn.

That won't last two foggy mornings.

The distance to the next milepost depends on the mud in the road.

Whenever I start wishing my life away. (Possible answer to: "When am I getting a pony?")

You can't hurry up good times by waiting for them.

Time to go lay the ole frame down. *Brenda Parker Anderson

Dearly Departed

The gophers are nibbling at his toes. *Adele McCall

Dead as iced catfish.

Deader than a doornail.

Graveyard dead.

Killed it dead. *Gil Little

Verse Eight:

Goodbye

Church is finally letting out.

Don't take any wooden nickels.

Don't let the door hit ya' where the good Lord split ya'.

That about puts the rag on the bush.

Time to piss on the fire and call in the dogs.

Well, let me get on about my rat killin'. *Ann Coleman Thames

Y'all come back now, ya' hear?

Book Two: The Collection of Southern Sayings by Category

Argumentative

She could start an argument in an empty house.

They would yank out a stop-sign to argue with the hole.

They would argue with a stoplight. (Or neon sign)

Bellyaching

Don't get your bowels in an uproar, your kidneys in a downpour and your liver in a jar.

Don't get your panties in a wad.

Don't anything hurt a duck but his bill.

Every path has a few puddles.

If a bullfrog had wings, he wouldn't bump his ass when he jumped.

If ifs and buts were candy and nuts, everyday would be Christmas.

If wishes were horses, then beggars would ride.

If your aunt had nuts she'd be your uncle.

It's not what it's worth; it's what it'll bring.

Most of the stuff people worry about ain't never gonna happen.

Not ever on a galloping horse.

The only thing fair in the world is the hair on a Norwegian albino's butt.

There's not much difference between a Hornet and a Yellow Jacket if they're in your clothes.

Wish in one hand and shit in the other and see which one fills up first. (Or spit)

Blue

I can't win for losing.

I feel like a banjo. Everybody's picking on me.

I feel like the last pea at pea-time.

I feel lower than a bow-legged caterpillar.

I'm lower than a snakes belly in a wagon rut.

I'm the red headed step child.

If momma ain't happy – ain't nobody happy.

Lower than an ankle bracelet on a flat-footed pigmy.

Messed up like a kite in a hail storm!

Sad as cucumber.

Sucking hind teat.

Swinging my legs from a dime.

Busy

As busy as a church fan in dog days.

Busier than a 2-dollar whore on nickel night.

Busier than a blind dog in a meat house.

Busier than a blind man at a striptease!

Busier than a cat burying shit on a marble floor.

Busier than a moth in a mitten!

Busier than a one-armed monkey with two peckers.

Busier than a one-armed paper hanger with jock itch.

Busier than a one-legged man in a butt kicking contest.

Busier than a set of jumper cables at a Mexican funeral.

Busier than ants at a picnic.

Busy as a cat on a hot tin roof.

Busy as a stump-tailed cow in fly season.

I don't have time to cuss the cat.

I got more things to do than a dog with fleas.

I'm as busy as a farmer with one hoe and two rattlesnakes.

I'm up to my ass in alligators.

I'm busier than a borrowed mule.

I'm running around like a chicken with its head cut off.

Capable

Handier than a shirt pocket.

He could talk the dogs off of a meat truck.

I wouldn't trade her for a farm in Georgia.

I'm just a country boy. (Warning: don't play poker with this one.)

No flies on them.

She could sell salt to a snail. *Sarah Ash

Smart as a whip.

Smart as a tree full of owls.

Useful as a prefabricated post hole.

Charming

Prettier than a mess of fried catfish.

Prettier than a speckled pup under a wagon with his tongue hanging out.

Pretty as a spotted horse in a daisy pasture.

She had a butt like a forty-dollar mule. (Or government mule)

She's hot as a 2 dollar pistol.

She has legs to lunch box! *Melissa and Randy Hilton

She's cuter than pig nipples.

She's pretty as a speckled pup.

She's finer than frog hair split eight ways!

Chatty

As full of wind as a corn-eating horse.

Ask him the time and he'll tell you how to build a watch.
(Clock)

Could lick a skillet in the kitchen from the front porch.

Full of gas with nowhere to go.

Got tongue enough for ten rows of teeth.

He's a manure salesman with a mouthful of samples.

He blew in on his own wind.

He could talk the gate off its hinges.

He could talk the hide off a cow.

He could talk the legs off a chair.

He shoots off his mouth so much he must eat bullets for breakfast.

He will talk your ear off.

He'd drive a wooden Indian crazy.

He'll tell you how the cow ate the cabbage.

He's a live dictionary.

He's got a ten-gallon mouth.

Her mouth is going like a bell clapping out of a goose's ass.

His tongue wags at both ends.

If bullshit were music, he'd have a brass band!

She beats her own gums to death.

She could talk a coon right out of a tree.

She speaks ten words a second, with gusts to fifty.

So windy he could blow up an onion sack.

Their mouth runs like a boarding house toilet.

She was vaccinated with a Victrola.

Windy as a sack full of farts.

Confused

A cat always blinks when hit on the head with a sledgehammer.

As lost as Hogan's goat.

Confused as a fart in a fan factory.

He doesn't know whether to check his ass or scratch his watch.

He was like a blind dog in a meat house.

He was so confused he didn't know his ass from his elbow.

He's a tree high squirrel.

He's more confused than a turtle on the center stripe.

I didn't know if I should shit and go blind or fart and close one eye.

I don't know if I found my rope or lost my cow. *Holly Crim Springer

I felt like a monkey trying to do a math problem.

Like an Amish electrician.

Like a bagel in a bucket of grits.

Like a fart in a skillet.

Like a monkey humping a football.

Lost as last year's Easter egg.

Lost ball in high weeds.

My tongue got in front of my eyetooth and I couldn't see what I was saying.

Running around like a chicken with its head cut off.

Courtship

Ashes to ashes and dust to dust, if it wasn't for women our

peckers would rust.

Bait the cow to catch the calf.

Candy is dandy but liquor is quicker.

Don't blame the cow when the milk gets sour.

Don't he think he's cock o' the hen-house.

Even a dog knows the difference between being stumbled
over and kicked.

Give me some sugar.

Go for the ugly early and you'll never go home alone.

sHe's got a thumping gizzard for a heart.

He is welcome to eat Ritz crackers in my bed anytime.

Hornier than a two-peckered billy goat.

I am sugar in your hand.

I couldn't get nailed in a wood workshop.

I didn't take her to raise.

I don't know her from Adam's house cat.

I'd fight tigers in the dark with a switch for him.

I'd jump on that like a duck on a June-bug.

I've got church in the morning. (Hurry up)

If I had that swing on my back porch id ride it every night.

If it has tires or testicles it's gonna give you trouble.

If promises were persimmons, possums could eat good at her place.

If you can sleep with 'em, I can eat with 'em!

It's not too pretty for nice, but it's great for good.

In that skirt, her butt looks like two Indian boys fighting under a blanket.

Like putting gas in a car that you've already wrecked.

Marriage is an expensive way for a man to get free laundry.

Marry in haste, repent in leisure.

Rooster one day, a feather duster the next.
She's got her trotting harness on.

She's anybody's dog that will hunt with her.
She had a voice that would chip paint.

She was all over that like a bad rash on a big ass.

She was batting her eyes like a toad in a hailstorm.

She's like a booger that you can't thump off.

She's limber as a dishrag.

Sure as the vine twines 'round the stump, you are my darlin' sugar lump.

That's a hard dog to keep on the porch.

The more you cry, the less you have to piss.

Trouble with a milk cow is she won't stay milked.

Wasn't nothin' between him and the Lord but a smile.

Well, ain't he just the tom-cat's kitten?

What good for the goose is good for the gander.

Why buy the cow if you get the milk for free.

Women have to be more beautiful than smart, because men see better than they think.

You can catch more bees with honey.

You can't ride two horses with one ass.

You could give her Heaven and Earth – she'd still want a pea patch in Hell.

Dearly Departed
Dead as iced catfish.

Deader than a doornail.

Graveyard dead.

Killed it dead. *Gil Little

Resting in peace in the marble orchard.

The gophers are nibbling at his toes. *Adele McCall

Dimwits

A few clowns short of a circus.

A few fire-logs short of a cord.

A few fries short of a Happy Meal.

A tree stump in a Louisiana swamp has a higher IQ.

About as sharp as a rat turd on both ends.

Couldn't get into college with a crowbar.

Didn't have sense enough to pound sand into a rat hole.

Doesn't have sense God gave an animal cracker. *Lucie May Thompson

Dumb as a cat grooming itself in the middle of a dog festival.

Dumb enough for twins.

Dumber than a box (bag, or barrel) of dirt. (Hair, hammers, doorknobs or rocks)

Dumber than a road lizard. (Brick, cabbage, fencepost, stump)

Dumber than a football bat.

'Et up with the dumb-ass.

Empty as a winter rain barrel.

Empty wagons make the loudest noise. (Or rain barrels)

Engine is running, but nobody is driving.

He ain't got the sense he was born with.

He ain't exactly setting the woods on fire.

He ain't got the sense the good Lord gave a billy goat (goose).

He ain't got the sense to lead a blind goose to shit.

He ain't the brightest Crayola in the box.

He ain't the sharpest knife (or spoon) in the drawer.

He couldn't hit the broad side of a barn with a sail cat.

He couldn't hit the ground if he fell twice!

He doesn't know "come here" from "sic 'em."

He got stuck behind the door when they were handing out brains.

He hasn't got the sense God gave a pregnant peanut.

He thought Grape Nuts was a venereal disease.

He thought Peter Pan was a bed pan.

He was casket sharp! *Kevin Spencer

He's a few dogs shy of a hunt.

He's duller than a three-watt light bulb in a power outage.

He's got all the smarts God gave a duck's butt.

He's so dumb he couldn't find his ass with two hands and a flashlight.

He's so dumb he couldn't piss his name in the snow.

He's so dumb he couldn't spell cat if you spotted him the "c" and the "t".

He's so dumb he thinks Johnny Cash is a pay toilet.

He's so dumb they had to burn down the school just to get him out of third grade.

His brain rattles around like a BB in a boxcar.

His cornbread ain't done.

His porch light is out.

If brains were dynamite we wouldn't have enough to blow his nose.

If brains were leather, he wouldn't have enough to saddle a June bug.

If I put his brain in a gnat's butt, it would fly backwards.

If brains were lard, he couldn't grease up a skillet.
If that boy had an idea it would die of loneliness.

Just about half-smart.

Nice house, but no one's home.

Plumb "et up" with the dumb ass.

Sharp as a bag of wet mice. (Or wet liver)

Sharp as a cue ball. (Balloon, lightbulb, or marble)

So dumb he couldn't pour piss out of a boot with the instructions written on the heel.

So dumb he took a duck to a chicken fight.

Strong like a bear and smart like a tractor.

That boy ain't the smartest peanut in the toilet.

That boy's the nearest nothing. *Bob Nelson

Their brains in a thimble would roll like road apples in a bushel basket.

They are nine dimes short of a dollar.

They think Cheerios are doughnut seeds!

Won't get bowlegged by totting his brains.

Your brain on the head of a pin would roll around like a BB on a six-lane highway.

Dirt Poor

Ain't got a pot to piss in let alone a window to throw it out of.

As poor as field mice.

Broke as the Ten Commandments.

I am so broke I can't buy a flea on a motorcycle jacket. *Marie Anderson Vaughn

I couldn't buy a hummingbird on a string for a nickel.

I couldn't jump over a nickel to save a dime.

If a trip around the world cost a dollar, I couldn't get to

the state line.

If I stepped on a worn out dime I could tell you whether it's heads or tails.

My brothers and I had to ride double on a stick horse.

Poor as Job's turkey.

So poor I've got to fart to have a cent.

So poor he'd have to borrow money to buy water to cry with.

Thick in the middle and poor on both ends.

They ate so many armadillos, grandpa rolls up into a ball when a dog barks.

Too poor to paint, too proud to whitewash.

Too poor to pay attention.

We were so poor I had a tumbleweed as a pet.

We were so poor we had to move every time the rent came due. *Tom Owens

We were so poor we had to use a 'possum as a yard dog. *Tom Owens

Effortless

A can of corn and a pop fly.

Ain't no hill for a climber.

Ain't no thang but a chicken wang (wing).

Easier than falling off a greasy log.

Elders

A little long in the tooth.

Grandpa goes to bed with the chickens.

He ain't sawing logs, he's clearing brush. (Snoring loudly)

He was old back when Jesus was a boy.

He's about two years older than baseball.

He's as old as Methuselah.

If he had one more wrinkle, he could screw his hat on.

Older than the mountains and got twice as much dust.

Only thing alive at that house with all its teeth is the termites.

She has enough wrinkles to hold an eight day rain.

They've been around since dirt was new.

Way back when I was knee-high to nothing.

When grandpa was born, the Dead Sea was just sick.

Exclamations!

Bless your pea picking little heart!

Cotton-picker!

Damn Yankees!

Don't rush on my account! (Please leave!)

Don't that take the rag off of the bush!

Snap my garters!

Don't that just beat all you ever stepped in!

For lands sake! *Kathy Hilliard Sanders

Gad night a livin'!

Gather at the River!

Going to Hell in a hand-basket!

Good God almighty!

Good heavenly days!

Great day in the morning!

Hellfire and damnation!

Hells' bells!

Hissy fit with a tail on it.

I am losing my religion!

I declare! (Also: I do declare.)

I swannie.

I'll be dipped in shit and rolled in cracker crumbs!

I'll fly away Ole Glory!

If it ain't bedbugs it's piss ants! *Kay Humphreys Abernathy

In all my born days!

Jesus H. Christ on a Popsicle stick!

Katie bar the door!

Lord help me over the fence! *Mandy Graham

Lord only knows – and he ain't telling!

My stars and garters!

Piss on that step ant! (We enjoy swapping letters in vulgar words) *Wade Hampton Sutherland

Quit hollering down the rain·

Shit fire and save the matches!

Stop that carrying on!

Swat my hind with a melon rind!

That makes my ass want a dip of snuff·

That is just sor-reee· (Sorry)

That sticks in my craw·

That's a fine how de' ya' do!

Well color me stupid!

Well cut off my legs and call me shorty!

Well hush my mouth!

Well I never!

Well knock me down and steal my teeth!

Well slap my head and call me silly!

Well, go to war Miss Mitchell!

Well, thank you Billy Sunday!

What does that have to do with the price of tea in China?

What in tarnation!

You scratch my back and I'll scratch yours.

Excuse Me

I got to go see a man about a dog. (cow, goat or horse).

I got to pee like a crippled goat.

I got to piss like a Russian race horse at the Kentucky derby
with a glue truck chasing.

I have to drop the Browns off at the Super Bowl.

I hear a bull pissing on a flat rock.

I'm going to see the turtle take to water. *Kevin Spencer

My eyeballs are floating.

The only thing we got to fear is a public toilet seat.

Glad

Finer than frog's hair.

Grinning like a mule eating briers over a barbwire fence.

Grinning like a possum eating grits out of a light socket.

Happier than a tornado in a trailer park.

Happier a preacher's son at a biker-babe rally!

Happier than a water spaniel on a bare leg.

Happier than a dead pig in the sunshine.

Happier than a gopher in soft dirt.

Happier than a June-bug on a tomato plant.

Happier than a pig in slop.

Happier than a possum in the corn-crib.

Happier than a puppy with two peckers.

Happier than a woodpecker in a lumber yard!

Happy as a tick on a fat dog.

Happy as a biker at the buffet.

I haven't had this much fun since pigs ate my brother.

I'm as giddy as a school girl on prom night.

I'm happier than a mule in a pickle patch.

I'm so tickled I can't get my leg down.

If I was any happier I'd be twins.

If things get any better, I may have to hire someone to help me enjoy it.

Still kickin' but not high, still floppin' but can't fly. (Fair to middling) *Audrey Wright

Goodbye

Church is out.

Don't take any wooden nickels.

Don't let the door hit ya' where the good Lord split ya'.

Let's head for the wagon yard.

Holler if you need me.

It's time to heat up the bricks.

It's time to put the chairs in the wagon.

It's time to swap spit and hit the road.

Keep your saddle oiled and your gun greased.

Let's blow this pop stand.

Let's light a shuck.

Let's put some lipstick on this pig!

That about puts the rag on the bush.

That's all she wrote.

Time to piss on the fire and call in the dogs.

Well, let me get on about my rat killin'. *Ann Coleman Thames

Y'all come back now, hear?

Gossip

Drove her ducks to a poor puddle.

Everything she's got is right on the showroom floor.

Fast with his hat and slow with his money.

He's gone back on his raisin'.

He got weaned from sucking eggs.

He is as country as cornflakes. (Or corn)

He'd complain if you hung him with a new rope.

He'd gripe with a ham under each arm.

He's a hard dog to keep under the porch.

He's the cream of the crap, and the crap of the cream.
*He's the kind of guy who'll put a rattlesnake in your pocket
and ask you for a light.*

*Her ass looks like a couple of squirrels fighting over an acorn
in a gunny sack.*

Her jeans are so tight; you can see Washington grinning on the quarter in her back pocket.

His pants were so tight that if he farted, he'd blow his boots off.

I hate his stomach for carrying his guts.

It must be jelly because jam don't shake like that.

Jesus loves him, but that's about it.

Just between you, me, and the fence post.
Lives like a fighting cock.

Those two ladies at the salad bar look like two Buicks fighting for a parking place.

Momma's baby - Daddy's maybe.

Rabbit running through the briar patch and don't know which one stuck it. *Connie Beckwith Self

She always looks like she stepped out of a band box.

She could depress the devil.

She could make a preacher cuss.

She looks like death sitting on tombstones hatching haints.
*Rita Langley Moran Harris

She's a caution.

She's an iron hand in a velvet glove. *Marian Dulaney Fortner

She's got more nerve than Carter's got Liver Pills. (The FDC removed "liver" from the name in 1961.)

She's must have eleven-teenth kids.

She's so stuck up, she'd drown in a rainstorm.

She's so sweet; sugar wouldn't melt in her mouth

She's wilder than a fifth ace.

She's as welcome as a skunk at a lawn party.

She's as wild as a peach orchard boar.

She's been "storked". (Pregnant)

She's dancing in the hog trough.

She's itching for something she won't scratch for.

She's sitting below the salt.

Sorry as a two dollar watch.

Still wet behind your ears.

That girl is like a doorknob. (Everyone gets a turn.)

That woman learned how to whisper in a saw mill.

The higher the hair, the closer to God. *Christi Whitsell Hawkins

They ate supper before they said grace.

They never could set horses.

Wasn't nothin' between him and the Lord but a smile.

Wild as a mink.

You can't hold water. (Keep a secret)

Greetings

Aren't you precious?

Bright-eyed and bushy-tailed.
Better than snuff and ain't half as dusty.

Did Ford stop making trucks? (Why so sad?)

Everything's chicken but the bill.

Fair to middlin'.

Fine as a frog's hair split up the middle and tied at both ends. (Or split three ways)

Gooder'n snuff (or grits).

Haven't seen you in a minute.

How's your Momma n 'em?

I'm all wool and a yard wide.

I'm hanging in there like loose teeth.

I'm keeping it between the ditches.

I'm doing as little as possible and the easy ones twice.

If I knew you were coming, I'd have baked a cake! *Mary Tubbs

Look what the cat drug up!

Set a spell.

We get along like a house on fire!

Went to the outhouse and the hogs ate him. (I don't know)

Who licked the red off your candy?

Who pissed in your Wheaties?

You little cotton-picker!

You're a sight for sore eyes.

Health

Fit as a Fiddle.

Happier than a pig in shit.

He's got a hitch in his get-a-long.

I am "et" up with it. (Consumed by)

I feel like a bag of smashed assholes.

I feel like I got eaten by a bear and shit off a cliff.

I'm bowed up like a Halloween cat.

I'm so sick I'd have to get better to die.

Like 5 gallons of shit in a 2 gallon bucket.

Right as rain.

She looks like she was rode rough and put away wet.

Sick as a dog passing peach pits.

Homely

About as sexy as socks on a billy goat.

As ugly as a stack of black cats with their tails cut off.

Beauty is only skin deep, but ugly goes right to the bone.

Born short and slapped flat.

He could scare a rat off a cheesecake.

His momma had to tie a pork chop around her neck to get

the dogs to play with them.

Has to sneak up on a fountain to get a drink.

He didn't get hit with the ugly stick; he got whooped with the whole forest!

He fell out of the ugly tree and hit every branch on the way down.

He looks like he has been suckin' a sow!

He looks like he was inside the outhouse when lightning struck.

He looks like something the dog has been keeping under the porch.

He looks like three pounds of ugly in a two-pound sack.

He stuck his finger in a light socket while his mama was beating him with an ugly stick.

He was so buck toothed he could eat an apple through a picket fence. (Or keyhole)

He's so ugly his cooties have to close their eyes.

He's so cross-eyed he can stand on the front porch and count chickens in the backyard.

Her behind is big as the Buckeye fence. *Kevin Spencer

Her hair looks like it caught on fire and somebody put it out with a brick.

Her hair was fried, dyed and laid to the side.

His eyes were so crossed; he could keep one eye on the snake and look for a stick to kill him with the other eye. *Alan Dearman

His mother borrowed another baby for baptism.

I wonder what she would charge to haunt a house.

If you fell into a pond, you could skim off ugly for a week.

It takes a whole lotta liquor to like her.

Last time I saw a mouth like that it had a bit in it. (Or hook)

Looks like he sorts bobcats for a living.

Looks like he was pulled through a knothole backwards.

Looks like ten miles of bad road.

Mama takes him everywhere she goes so she doesn't have to kiss him goodbye.

Plain as a river slug. *Charles Smith

She could scare the bulldog off a meat truck.

She had a face so ugly she wore out two bodies.

She looks like her face caught fire and somebody put it out with an ice pick.

She looks like she got hit in the face with a sackful of bent nickels.

She looks like she got hit in the face with rock salt.

She looks like she plays goalie for a dart team.

She looks like she ran a forty-yard dash in a thirty-yard gym.

She was so ugly she looked like her face caught fire and someone beat it out with a track shoe.

She's ugly enough to stop an eight-day clock.

So ugly he'd scare a buzzard off a gut pile.

So ugly she'd make a freight train take a dirt road.

So ugly they had to trick or treat over the telephone.

So ugly when she was a baby her mom fed her with a slingshot.

Somebody broke the ugly stick over his head.

Stump-hole ugly.

That baby is so ugly, when he was born the doctor slapped his Mama.

That boy is so ugly he couldn't get laid in a whore house with a fist full of hundreds.

That face might not stop a clock, but it'd sure raise Hell with watches.

Their momma had to be drunk to breastfeed them!

They couldn't hem up a pig in a corner.

They'd knock a buzzard off a gut wagon.

They have a face for radio.

Uglier than a lard bucket full of armpits.

Ugly as a mud fence daubed with tadpoles.

Ugly as homemade sin. (Or lye soap)

Ugly enough to stop a bucket of snot in mid-air.

How Much?

A country as corn. (Or cornflakes)

About as much fun as a warm bucket of calf slobber.

As happy as a possum in a persimmon tree.

As slick as cat shit on linoleum.

As welcome as an outhouse breeze.

Barefooted as a yard dog.

Better than a sharp stick in the eye.

Bleeding like a stuck pig.

Bowed up like a banty rooster.

Brave as a bigamist.

Brave as the first man to eat an oyster.

Brave enough to eat in the boomtown saloon.

By the skin of my teeth.
Clean as a hound's tooth.

Common as goat nuts.

Cooler than the other side of the pillow.

Country as a baked bean sandwich!

Dark as a sack of black cats.

Dark as the inside of a cow.

Deaf in one ear and can't hear out of the other.

Even a blind man on a galloping horse could see it.

Flashy as a rat with a gold tooth.

Flatter than a fritter.

Forty going north.

Funny as a piss ant floating on his back with an erection hollering for the draw bridge to open.

Going at it like killing snakes.

Good enough for state work.

Green as a gourd.

Grinning like a possum eating a sweet potato.

Harder than a wedding pecker.

He ain't sawing logs, he's clearing brush. (Snoring loudly.)

He looked like a pig on ice.

He talks like he's got a mouthful of mush.

He thinks he's the best thing since sliced bread.

He thinks the sun come up just to hear him crow.

He was so fat it was easier to go over top of him than around him.

He was the turd in the punchbowl.

He's so deaf, he can't hear himself fart.

He's so scared you couldn't drive a wet watermelon seed up his butt with a sledge hammer.

He's so thin-skinned, it's just barely enough to keep him from bleeding to death.

He's scratched up worse than a blind berry picker.

He's shaking like an old dog shittin' logging chains. (Hammer handles or peach seeds)

He's so country he thinks a seven-course meal is a possum and a six-pack.

Heavier than a dead preacher.

High as giraffe nuts.

I bought it for a song and you can sing it yourself.

I locked that thing up tighter than Casey's nuts.

I was never like this until I was born.

I was stuck hub deep to a Ferris wheel.

I'm sweating like a whore in church.

I'm up shit creek without a paddle.

I'm just hanging out like a hair in a biscuit.

I'm out like a fat kid in dodge-ball.

I'm prouder of that than a pup with his first flea.

If that don't tickle your fancy, I'll kiss your ass until your hat flies off. *Jeri Hale

It was hanging open like a pea-coat sleeve.

It's a right far piece from here.

It's over yonder in the edge of nothing.

It's quieter than a mouse pissing on cotton.

It's more than I can say grace over.

Just a hop skip and a jump. *Judy Noble

Knee high to a grasshopper.

Like a garlic milkshake. (Smooth and strong).

Like a polecat at a camp meeting.

Like a popcorn fart in Hell. (Ignored)

Like a rooster in an empty hen-house. (Frustrated)

Like a rubber nosed woodpecker in a petrified forest. (Frustrated)

Long as a month of Sundays. (Amusement was once forbidden on Sundays.)

Looks greener than gourd guts.

Looks like Hell with everyone out to lunch.

More fun than a sackful of kittens.

More than one way to skin a cat.
No higher than corn and no lower than taters.

Not big enough to cuss the cat in.

Not too pretty for nice, but great for good.

Now we're cookin' with gas!

Over yonder at the edge of nothing.

Pert near, but not plumb.

Rough as a cob.

Rougher than a pulp wood truck in a cotton patch. *Hugh Murray

Scarce as a hen's teeth.

Scarce as deviled eggs after a church picnic.

Screamed like a mashed cat.

Sharper than a mother-in-law's tongue.

She didn't say "pea turkey squat".

She was so tall she could hunt geese with a rake.

She wouldn't go to a funeral unless it was theirs.

She's so deaf, she can't hear a fart in a jug.

Slapped him like a red-headed stepchild.

Slick as an eel.

Slick as snot on a goat's glass eye.

Slicker than a chased greased hog.

Slicker than a minnow's pecker.

Slicker than deer guts on a door knob. *Mavis Morton

Slicker than otter snot.

Slicker than shit through a tin horn.

Slicker than snot and smashed bananas.

Smaller than a skeeter peter.

Smaller than a tick turd.

Smiling like a goat in a briar-patch.

Smoother than a hairy nipple on wax day.

So deep in jail he'll have to be fed beans with a sling-shot!

So sore can't touch it with a powder puff.

Sober as a judge.

Squirming like a worm in hot ashes. (Or a hot brick)

Stout as a mule.

Strong as bear's breath.

Stuck so bad I needed a four wheel drive helicopter to pull my truck out.

Sweating like a cow in a pasture full of bulls. * Gigi Goss Lewis

Tail up and stinger out.

Tender as a judge's heart.

That fits tighter than socks on a rooster.

That is just the cat's pajamas.

That kid ain't knee-high to a duck.

That's lower then quail shit in a wagon rut!

That's more exciting than snuff and not near as dusty.

That's better than sliced bread.

That's close enough for government work.

The personality of a dishrag.

There were so many people, you couldn't stir 'em with a stick.

They could worry the horns off a billy goat.

They live so far out they have to pipe in sunshine.

They lived so far out in the country that the sun set between their house and town.

Thick as flies on a dog's back.

Thicker than fiddlers in Hell.

Tighter than a rat's ass in a keyhole.

Tighter than a skeeter's ass in a nosedive.

Weak as dishwater.

Were closer than two roaches on a bacon bit.

Whiter than a hound dog's tooth.

Wound tighter than a three day clock. (Or two dollar watch)

Written on the heel.

You can see it clearer than balls on a tall dog!

You can't sling a cat without hitting one.

You look like 10 pounds of smashed assholes in a 5 pound sack.

You look like something the cat dragged in and the kittens

didn't want.

You're so blind you could miss a crawdad playing cards with Ray Charles.

You're swinging that driver like a washer woman.

Hungry
I am so hungry I can see biscuits walking on crutches! *
Janice Box-Franklin

I could eat the ass end out of a rag doll.

I'm so hungry I could eat the north end of a south-bound goat. (mule or polecat)

I'm so hungry my belly button is sticking out of my butt.

I'm so hungry, every time I swallow my asshole says thank you.

I'm so hungry, I'd eat the balls off a low flying duck!

I'm as hungry as a tick on a turnip.

I'm so hungry my backbone is snapping at my belt buckle.

So hungry my belly thinks my throat's been cut.

Insults

Almost as smart as people say he thinks he is.

Big hat, no cattle.

Cain't, never could.

Call him an idiot and you'll insult all the idiots in the world.

Couldn't find his own ass with both hands stuck in his back pockets.

Couldn't punch his way out of a wet paper bag.

Give me a fly-snapper and I'll help you kill it. (Comment about a hairdo.)

He's so low down he could crawl under a snake's belly.

His family tree ain't got branches.

I don't think he has enough chlorine in his gene pool.

I wouldn't walk across the street to piss on him if he was on fire.

Is that your head or did your neck throw up?

I've stepped over better than you looking for a place to piss.

If I had a dog as ugly as you, I'd shave his butt and make him walk backwards.

If I want your opinion I will unscrew the top of your head

and dip it out. *Fred Doane

If a gnat had your brain it would fly backwards.

If stupid could fly, you'd be a jet.

If you can't run with the big dogs, stay under the porch.

If you had any brains you would be dangerous. *Gail Bouldin

Not worth the powder and shot it'd take to blow you to church.

That truck couldn't pull a fat baby off a tricycle.

Fish stinks from the head down too.

The last time I saw a mouth that big it had a hook in it.

The only thing that separates you from white trash is your rich husband.

When you die you're gonna have to rise up to find Hell.

Why don't you take a flying f#ck at a rolling doughnut!

You ain't through climbing fool's hill yet.

You are full of gas with nowhere to go.

You ain't nothing but a piss ant in the big ant hill of life.

You can put a coat and tie on a turd, but it's still gonna be a turd.

You can't make chicken salad out of chicken shit.

You could start an argument in an empty house.

You know I wouldn't shit you - you're my favorite turd.

You now as much about that (any topic) as a hog knows about Sunday. *Tom Owens

You shouldn't be hunting anything smarter than you.

You smell like you want to be left alone.

You're like a bad penny.

You're as smart as you are good looking - and that ain't saying much.

Your momma should have killed you and sold the milk.

Intoxicated

Drunk as Cooter Brown. (Cooter Brown stayed drunk during the entire Civil War)

Drunker than a bicycle. *Kathy Hilliard Sanders

He was drunker than a skunk.

He's so drunk he couldn't hit the floor with his hat.

Higher than a Georgia pine.

Three sheets in the wind.

Tore up from the floor up.

Torn up like a New Jersey train wreck.

You have a hollow leg.

Lazy

Born in the middle of the week and looking both ways for Sunday.

Dead flies wouldn't fall off of him.

Follows the shade around the house.

He's got molasses in his britches.

He wouldn't hit a lick with a snake.

He moves like the lice is falling off him.

He wouldn't say "shit" if he had a mouthful of it.

He's so lazy he calls the dog inside to see if it's raining.

Sitting there like a bump on a log. (Also: Wart on a frog.)

So lazy he wouldn't work in a pie factory as a taster.

Luck - Both Kinds

A wing and a prayer.

Even a blind hog finds an acorn every once in a while.

Good Luck says, "Open your mouth and shut your eyes."

I could fall into a barrel of teats and come out sucking my thumb.

If he fell into an outhouse he'd come up smelling like a rose.
He could sit on the fence and the birds would feed him.

He's riding the gravy train with biscuit wheels.

It doesn't take a prophet to predict bad luck.

The sun don't shine on the same dog's tail all the time.

You must not be holding your mouth right. (Or living your life right)

Momma Said

A body can't get a minute's peace in this house.

A hard head makes a soft behind.

Act like you got some raisin'.

A little bird told me.

Better not let your shirt tail touch your back until you get it done. *Tom Owens

Better tend to your own knittin'.

Close the door, you're letting the flies out. (Or in)

Don't be ugly. (Mean)

Don't get your cows running.

Don't look at me in that tone of voice. *Ann Fassetta

Don't monkey with that.

Don't sass back.

Don't worry about closing the barn door now once the cows got out.

Don't worry that. (Leave it be.)

Don't you make eyes at me.

Faint of heart never won fair maiden.
Get back on your lily pad.

Get your butt off your shoulders!

Getting too big for your britches.

Go cut me a switch.

Go on and run - y'all gotta come home sometime.

God blessed the dirt; the dirt will not hurt, put it in your mouth and let it work.

Has the cat got your tongue?

Have clean drawers on - you may get in a car accident. *Fran Hart and Gail Bouldin

He buttered his britches.

Hold your horses.

I am fixin' to lose my religion.

I brought you into this world - I'll take you out. *Eddy Hays

I didn't just fall off the turnip truck. (Or) I didn't just ride in on a load of pumpkins.

I got one nerve left and you are jumping all over it.

I love you like a bushel and a peck, and a hug around your neck. *Sheila Rast Wilson

If you're gonna be stupid, you better be tough.

If you fall out of that tree and break your leg don't come running to me. *Phil Tillman

I love you so much I could eat you up blood raw with no salt! *R Mike Walker

I see Christmas!

*I would rather go to a shit slinging than be seen wearing something like that. *Linda Walker Switzer*

*If you're going to be a turd go lay in the yard.
If you mess with crap, you get crap on you.*

I'll knock you into the middle of next week looking both ways for Sunday!

*I'll slap a knot on your head it will take a bulldozer to smooth out. *Tom Owens*

*I'm fixin' to put some nickel knots on your head. *Kathy Hilliard Sanders*

I'm gonna slap you so hard when you quit rollin' your clothes will be outta style.

I'm gonna jerk you bald!

If you can go out on Saturday night you can go to church on Sunday morning.

If you keep an aspirin between your legs you cannot get pregnant.

Instead of saying "hey", save it - you might marry a jackass one day.

*Is this what you wanna be doing when Jesus comes back?
Samantha Reed

It's gonna take a rusty corncob to get this dirt off you.
*Terri Richards Knight

If your jobs are small and your rewards seem few, remember
the mighty oak was once a nut like you.

Just sit there and sip your tea. *Mariechen Woodworth
McGruder

Keep it up and you're gonna be sitting at the right foot of
the Devil. *Andrea Jenea Bobo

Kids could break a second-hand anvil with a turkey feather.

Let the hair go with the hide.

Little pitchers have big ears.

Make sure you wash where the Yankee shot you. (Navel)
*Lynn Poor

Me and you are about to have a "come to Jesus" meeting.

Monkey see monkey do.

No matter where you go, there you are.
Pretty is as pretty does.

Put on your big boy britches.

Quit acting like your daddy's people.

Quit going around your ass to get to your elbow.

Raise that window down. (Yes! "down")

Raising kids is like being pecked to death by a chicken.

Stop jumping around like piss-ants on a hot griddle.

Stop that crying before I give you something to cry about.

Tell the truth and shame the Devil.

That boy is a poster child for birth control.

That lie is gonna split Hell right open. *Andrea Jenea Bobo

That's not sweet. (Don't be ugly)

That's tacky — you're not leaving the house in that.

That's your red wagon to pull. *Lisa McGee

Your barn door's open and the mule is trying to run.

The higher a monkey climbs the more he shows his ass.

The Lord greased your butt and slid you down a rainbow.
(Answer to the facts of life) *Kathleen Gallagher Bishop

The proof is in the pudding.

There's a dead cat on the line. (I don't believe you)
*Angela Smith

This ain't the Governor's ball you're dressing for.

Two buzzards bumped butts and you fell out. (Answer to the facts of life)

Well, now, little lady.

What in the Sam Hill is going on?

Why, bless your pea-picking little heart.

Y'all could tear up a ball bearing (or railroad track) with a rubber mallet.

You are acting like a cat's Aunt Jane. *Dan Walker

You're eating like a field hand.
Y'all are noisy enough to wake the dead.

You are wild as a March hare.

You can't fool God and you can't fool me! *Susan Stafford Buck

You can just get glad in the same britches you got mad in.

You have something in your mouth that I wouldn't hold in my hand. *Kathleen Gallagher Bishop

You make my butt want to dip snuff.

You're going to wool that baby to death.

You're gonna have old and new-monia dressed like that! (Pneumonia)

You're gonna mess with me and fall back in it!

You're looking at me like cow looking at a new gate. *Rusty
Gardner

You're the spitting image of your mother/father.

Your face is gonna freeze like that!

You kids are standing around the kitchen like buzzards on a
gut wagon.

Nervous

As nervous as a long-tailed cat in a room full of rockers.

I'm shaking like a hound dog trying to shit a peach pit.

In between the devil and the deep blue sea.

Like a frog on the freeway with a busted jumper.

Like a porcupine in a balloon factory.

Like a spring lizard in a hen-house.

My nuts are drawn up so tight you couldn't reach them
with knitting needles.

Nervous as a bear caught with his head in the hive.

Nervous as a cow with a bucktooth calf.

Nervous as a whore in church.

That would twist the back of your crotch out.

Wound tighter than a new girdle.

You couldn't drive a toothpick up my ass with a sledgehammer.

No

Crow and corn can't grow in the same field.

Does a chicken have lips?

Hard sayin' not knowin'.

I don't know them from Adam's house cat.

I'd rather be in Hell with a broken back.

I'd rather have a tick in my navel.

I'd rather be beat with a sack of wet catfish.
I'd rather jump barefoot off a 6-foot step ladder into a 5 gallon bucket full of porcupines.

I'd rather sandpaper a bobcat's ass in a phone booth. *Derek Brewer

I'd rather stare at the sun with binoculars.

I'll be dipped in bacon fat before I do that.

I'll pay you when my coon gets fat.

In a pig's eye. (Or) When pigs fly.
I'm near about past going.

Like a kerosene cat in Hell with gasoline drawers on.

My dog sleeps in the garage, but it doesn't make him a truck. Or you can put your boots in the oven, but that don't make 'em biscuits.

That dog won't hunt.

That is too much pumpkin for a nickel.

That possum's on the stump!

That will go over go over like a pregnant pole-vaulter.

That's a gracious plenty.

You might as well shove your money up a wolf's ass and watch him run over the hill.

Odors
Gag a maggot!

It smelled like a flatulent pack mule.

It smelled worse than a dead skunk that just crawled out of another dead skunk's ass.

Smelled like two tomcats fighting.

Stronger than ten acres of garlic.

That could knock a buzzard off a gut wagon. (Or gag a maggot off)

That smells like the shithouse door on a shrimp boat.

That stinks to high heaven.

Plumpish

Fat people are harder to kidnap.

Fatter than the town dog. *Whitney Crow Smith

He's got Dunlap's disease - his belly done lapped over his belt.

He's got the furniture disease - his chest done fell into his drawers.

He's digging his grave with his spoon.

His ass must be hungry - it's trying to eat his pants.

If she were an inch taller she'd be round.

If somebody told her to "haul ass," she'd have to make two trips.

It takes two dogs to bark at her.

She didn't get a round mouth by eating square meals.

She's spread out like a cold supper.

The Piggy Wiggly hires a rodeo clown to distract him when grocery shopping.

They stepped up on the scale to be weighed, it said "To be continued."

Proverbs

A blacksnake knows the way to the hen's nest.

A blind horse doesn't fall when he follows the bit.

A blind mule ain't afraid of darkness.

A bumblebee is faster than a John Deere tractor.

A bull without horns can still smart.

A crooked cornstalk can still have a straight ear.

An empty wagon makes a lot of noise.

A full purse ain't half as good as an empty one is bad.

A gallant retreat is better than a bad last stand.

A good farmer stays acquainted with daybreak.

A guilty dog barks the loudest.

A guilty fox hunts his own hole.

A hole in your britches lets in a heap of uneasiness.
A miss is as good as a mile.

A mule can be tame at one end and wild at the other.

A new broom sweeps clean, but an old one knows where the dirt is.

A one-eyed mule can't be handled on the blind side.

A pig has enough arithmetic to take the shortest cut through a thicket.

A pullet can't roost too high for an owl.

A rabbit knows a fox track same as a hound does.

A sharp ax is better than big muscle.

A sleepy fisherman totes a light load home.

A sore back mule is a poor hand at guessing the weight of a sack of meal.

A whistling woman and a crowing hen never come to a very

good end.

A wink is as good as a nod, to a blind horse.

A worm is the only animal that can't fall down.

Ain't no point in beating' a dead horse - but then it can't hurt either.

All of the justice in the world isn't fastened up in the courthouse.

All the buzzards will come to the mule's funeral.

Always drink pure water -many get drunk from breaking this rule.

An old sow knows enough about figures to count her pigs.

Angleworms aren't anxious for the fish to bite.

Anyone can fly - it's the landing that will kill you.

Be like the old lady who fell out of the wagon. (Stay out of it.)

Beating a dead horse don't make it taste better.

Better gravy than no grease at all.

Better to keep your mouth shut and seem a fool than to open it and remove all doubt.

Between the bug and the Bee Martin, it ain't hard to tell which will get caught.

Birds of a feather flock together.

Buzzards and chickens come home to roost.

Church ain't over until the choir quits singing.

Corn makes more at the mill than it does in the crib.

Country fences need to be horse high, pig tight, and bull strong.

Do God's will - whatever the Hell it may be.

Don't argue with idiots, they will drag you down to their level and beat you with experience.

Don't bite off more than you can chew.

Don't corner something that you know is meaner than you.

Don't count your chickens until they hatch.

Don't ever wash a pig, you'll just get dirty, and the pig will enjoy it.

Don't fling away the empty wallet.

Don't get in a pissing contest with a polecat.

Don't go off with your pistol halfcocked.

Don't let the tail wag the dog.

Don't let your mouth overload your tail.

Don't start chopping until you've treed the coon.

Don't sweat the petty things – pet the sweaty things.

Don't take too big a start to jump a ditch.

Don't trade off a coonskin before you catch the coon.

Don't try to rake up the family secrets of every sausage you eat.

Don't worry about the mule going blind just load the wagon.

Don't hang your wash on someone else's line.

Don't judge folks by their relatives.

Don't name a pig you plan to eat.

Don't rile the wagon master.

Don't sell your mule to buy a plow.

Don't skinny dip with snapping turtles.

Drinking wine today, picking grapes tomorrow.

Early don't last long.

Eat the frog.

Every day is just a role of the dice, and snake eyes is just a way of life.

Every dog should have a few fleas.

Everything that goes around at night ain't Santa Clause.

Fattened hogs ain't in luck.

Folks on the rich bottom land stop bragging when the river rises.

Fools' names and fools' faces always appear in public places.
*David Gaddie

Good fences make good neighbors.

Crabgrass lines the path to the poorhouse.

Ground sparrows will see the snowstorm way off.

Grubbing roots softens a straw bed.

Hair of the dog is good for the bite.

Hard liquor and a hammer ought to fix that.

I'd take Heaven for the climate and Hell for the company.

If at first you don't succeed, use duct tape.

If duct tape doesn't fix it - then you're not using enough duct tape.

If God had intended for Texans to ski, he would have made bullshit white.

If you ain't the lead dog the scenery never changes.
If you buy a rainbow, don't pay cash for it.

If you can't race it or take it to bed, you don't need it.

If you cut your own firewood, it'll warm you twice.

If you don't have time to do it right when will you have time to do it over? *Vickie J Boulton

If you don't use your head, you might as well have two asses.

If you have to eat dirt, eat clean dirt.

If you have to eat two frogs, eat the big one first.

If you lie down with dogs, you'll get up with fleas.

If you're bound to hang — you won't drown.

It doesn't rain every time the pig squeals.

It doesn't take a very big person to carry a grudge.

It'll all come out wash day. *Carolyn Graham

It's easy to get off a bucking mule.

It's hard to fly with the eagles when you run around with

the turkeys.

It's better to be pissed off then pissed on.

Just because a chicken has wings doesn't mean it can fly.

Just do all you can do and let the rough end drag.

Keep skunks and bankers at a distance.

Lazy folks' stomachs don't get tired.

Let sleeping dogs lie.

Life is simpler when you plow around the stump.

Life is what you need, love is what you want.

Liquor talks mighty loud when it gets loose from the jug.

Live and learn, die and know it all.

Loading a wagon with hay isn't the quickest way to get religion.

Love many, trust few and always paddle your own canoe.

Make haste - there ain't no coming back. *Carolyn Slay-Jones

Make hay while the sun shines.

Many good cotton stalks get chopped by associating with weeds.

Meat fried before day won't last until night.

Never ask a barber if he thinks you need a haircut.

Never bring a knife to a gun fight.

Never climb an oak tree for pecans.

Never shake hands with a crayfish.

Never sign anything by neon.

Never to go snipe hunting twice.

Never trust a man too far who stays mad through Christmas week.

No matter what you do to a skunk, it still stinks.

Pigs don't know what a pen's for.

Pigs get fat; hogs get slaughtered.

Rails split before breakfast will season the dinner.

Rheumatism and happiness both get bigger if you keep telling folks.

Satan ain't scared of long sermons.

Satan loads his cannons with big watermelons.

Save the pacing mare for Sunday.

Scared money don't win.

Setting hens don't hanker fresh eggs.

Skin your own buffalo.

Soft ground tells a heap of tales.

Stump water won't cure the gripes.

Teachers, bankers, and owls sleep with one eye open.

Tell me what you need and I'll tell you how to get along without it.

That rooster makes more racket than the hen that laid the egg.

The Black Gum laughs at the Red Oak when the woodcutter comes around.

The bullfrog never makes a mistake when he starts singing.

The cotton patch doesn't care which way you vote.

The devil has no particular objection to Christmas.

The dinner bell's always in tune.

The hawk would like to get a job in the chicken yard keeping away the minks.

The jay-bird doesn't rob his own nest.

The man that always takes the shortest road to a dollar generally takes the longest road away from it.

The mosquito says grace too loud for his own good before getting ready.

The mule doesn't pull so well with a mortgage on his back.

The mule that chews up his own collar is fixing for a sore shoulder.

The otter would have more peace if his clothes weren't so fine.

The partridge that makes a nest in a wheat field won't be pestered by her chicks.

The quickest way to double your money is to fold it over and put it back in your pocket.

The rabbit is too honest to steal grapes, and the fox is too honest to steal cabbage.

The rabbit thinks experience costs too much if you get it from a trap.

The road to Hell is paved with good intentions.
The terrapin walks fast enough to go visiting.

The woodpile doesn't grow much on frosty nights.

There's more than one way to break a dog from sucking

eggs.

There's no need for pockets on a dead man's coat.

Those who know too much sleep under the hopper.

Throw it up to the wind and let the dust settle it. *Brenda Pafford

To know how country folks are doing, look at their barns, not their houses.

Tomorrow may be the carriage-driver's day for plowing.

Tomorrow's ash-cake is better than last Sunday's pudding.

Trying to understand some folks is like guessing at the direction of a rat hole underground.

Turnip tops don't tell you the size of the turnips.

Two can live as cheap as one if one don't eat.

Water meets it's own level. *Lucie May Thompson

What you can learn by boxing with a left-hander costs more than it's worth.

What you don't have in your head, you have to have in your feet.

When it takes half a sandwich to catch a catfish, let him alone.

When life gives you scraps, make a quilt.

When you find yourself in a hole – quit digging.

When you wallow with pigs, expect to get dirty.

Whip a horse with oats.

Words that soak best into ears are whispered.

You can catch more files with honey than with vinegar.

You can hide the fire, but what will you do with the smoke?

You can pick your friends and you can pick your nose – but you can't wipe your friends on your saddle.

You can sow in my field, but the crop will come up in yours, and you won't know how it got there.

You can't get blood from a turnip.

You can't judge the depth of a well by the handle of the pump.

You can't make a silk purse out of a sow's ear.

You can't tell much about a chicken pie until you get through the crust.

You can't get lard unless you boil the hog.

You can't have chicken salad without the chicken shit.

You can't unsay a cruel word.

You got to be 10% smarter than the equipment you're running.

You have to draw to catch.

You might as well die with the chills as with the fever.

You will go to Hell for lying just as well stealing.

You'll lose your grip if you put too much spit on your hands.

Scolding

I can tell you a thing or two about a thing or two.

I got a bone to pick with you.

I been to two hog callins', a goat roast, and a World's Fair and I still ain't never seen nothing like you!

If I say a hen dips snuff, you can look under her wing for the can. Or If I tell you a duck can pull a truck, then shut up and hook the sucker up.

Keep it up and I'll cancel your birth certificate.

Let me tell you how the cow ate the cabbage.

My cow died last night, so I don't need your bull.

Take the bit between your teeth.
The north wind knows all the cracks in the house.

This ain't my first rodeo.

When you got nothing to say, you say it.

Who's plucking this chicken, you or me?

You don't have a lick of sense!

Saints

A person to go to the well with.

He'll stand the hedge and take up the gap.

He's so honest you could shoot craps with him over the phone.

No weevils in his wheat.

Straight as a string.

You can bet the farm on it.

You can hang your hat on it.

You can take that to the bank.

Scrawny

A strong fart in a whirlwind would blow him away.

He looks wormy.

He sure is poor.

He swapped legs with a jaybird and got cheated out of a butt.

He could fall through his ass and hang himself.

He'd have to stand up twice to cast a shadow.

He's only got one stripe on his pajamas.

His pants had only one back pocket.

If she stood sideways and stuck out her tongue she'd look like a zipper.

She could tread water in a test-tube.

She's a carpenter's dream: flat as a board and ain't ever been nailed.

Shiftless

As much good as windshield wipers on a ducks butt. *Mark Overby

Ain't worth the wagon he rode in on. *Kay McPherson

About as useful as buttons on a dishrag.

Ain't worth the salt in her bread.

Ain't nothin' but a hound dog.

All hat and no cow.

Couldn't carry a tune in a bushel basket.
Couldn't herd ducks to water in front of a pond. *Jimmy Dale Johnson

Couldn't hit a bull in the ass with a bass fiddle.

Couldn't pour piss out of a boot with the instructions printed on the heel.

Couldn't teach a settin' hen to cluck.

Dumber than a barrel of spit and half as useful.

Handy as a cow on crutches.

He's a legend in his own mind.
He couldn't find his own ass with both hands stuck in his back pockets.

115

He couldn't hit the broad side of a barn if he was inside it.

He couldn't organize a pissing contest in a brewery.

He couldn't carry a tune in a bucket.

He couldn't hit his own ass with directions and a map.

He couldn't hit the water if he fell out the boat.

He's about as useful as a steering wheel on a mule

He's about as useless as a bent dog pecker.

He's no 'count.

He's about as handy as a back pocket on a shirt.

He's about as useful as a pogo stick in quicksand.

He's as useful as a tit on a boar hog. (Lightbulb, bullfrog or bicycle)

I need him like a tomcat needs a trousseau.

Like a milk pail under a bull.
If he had a third hand he'd need an extra pocket to stick it in.

Never set a river on fire.

Too mean for Jesus and too dumb for the Devil.

Useful as a bull at a square dance.

Useful as a screen door on a submarine.

Useful as a trap door on a canoe.

Useful as an ashtray on a motorcycle.

Useless as hen-shit on a pump handle.

Worthless as a sidesaddle on a sow.

Skinflint

Close chewer and tight spitter.

He knows every dollar by first name.

He squeaks when he walks.

He squeezes a quarter so tight the eagle screams.

He'd squeeze a nickel until the buffalo farts.

His ass squeaks when he walks.

He's tighter than a bull's ass at fly time.

He wouldn't pay a nickel to see a piss ant pull a freight train.

Tighter than a flea's ass over a rain barrel.

Tighter than a tick.

Tighter than bark on a tree.

Tighter than Dick's hatband.

When he walks over a penny his butt quivers.

When he smiles his eyes curl up.

Wouldn't give a nickel to see Jesus riding a bicycle.

Speed - Fast

Fast as all get out.

Fast as greased lightning.

Faster than a bee stung stallion.

Faster than a bell clapper in a goose's ass.

Faster than a cat can lick its ass.

Faster than a frog (also dog) shot through a barn.

Faster than a hot knife through butter.

Faster than a monkey on moonshine.

Faster than a striped assed ape.

Faster than green grass through a goose.

Like a duck on a June bug.

He can turn off the switch and jump in bed before it gets dark.

He ran like a scalded dog. (Haint or cat)

He ran like his feet were on fire and his butt was catching.

He ran outta there like a turpentine cat.

He went through that like Sherman went through Georgia.

I am off like a dirty shirt! *Fred Doane

It happened faster than a knife fight in a phone booth.

Like a dose of salts through a widow woman.

Quick as a politician's promise.

Running like the house is on fire.

Took off like Moody's goose.

Speed - Slow

He was moving so slow, dead flies wouldn't fall off of him.

He's slower than a two legged coon dog on a Monday morning.

Last hog to the trough.

Like a cat eating a grindstone.

Runs just like a candle.

She has two speeds. Slow and stop.

Slower than a herd of turtles stampeding through peanut butter.

Slower than a snail drunk on molasses crawling up an ice hill in January.

Slower than a Sunday afternoon.

Slower than cream rising on last year's buttermilk.

Slower than pond water.
Slower than molasses running uphill in January.

Slower than turtles racing in molasses.

We're off like a herd of turtles.

Stubborn
Dug in like an Appalachian tick.

Like a billy goat: hard head and stinking butt.

Stubborn as a blue nosed mule.

Surprised

Butter my butt and call me a biscuit!

Caught with your pants down.

I was as surprised as if a sheep had bit me.

If it'd been a snake it would have bit you.

Knock me over with a feather!
Like finding a feather on a frog.

Like finding a diamond in a billy goat's butt.

Makes a bulldog want to hug a ham. *Art Bowman

So surprised you could have knocked his eyes off with a stick.

Stick a paper umbrella up my butt and call me a hurricane.

That takes the cake. (Biscuit or gravy)

Well don't that beat a goose gobbling! *Mark Davis

Well, ain't that the cat's pajamas!

Well, shut my mouth!

Well, slap my head and call me silly!

Whatever cranks your tractor!

You scared the livin' day lights outta me.

Temperature

Cold as a banker's heart.

Cold as a frog's behind.

Cold as a frosted frog.

Colder than a mother-in-law's love.

Colder than a well digger's nappy. *Clara Delk Martin

Colder than day old penguin shit.

He's hotter than a July firecracker.

Hot as a depot stove.

Hotter n' Hell's basement on the day of reckoning.

Hotter than a $2 pistol.

Hotter than a billy goat with a blowtorch.

Hotter than a June bride.

Hotter than a setting hen in a wool basket in the summer.

Hotter than a three-balled tomcat.

Hotter than Satan's house-cat.

Hotter than the hinges of Hell.

Hotter than two hamsters farting in a wool sock.

I'm hotter than a tick on a dog's balls.

It's hotter than a biscuit

It's hotter than Satan's toenails in here! *Marcy Foster

Testy

Dills my pickle!

Don't rush on my account!

Duck Fit!

Fit to be tied!

Fly off the handle.

Go sit in the truck! (Get out of my way!)

He's got his tail up.

He's madder than a puffed toad.

I could chew up nails and spit out a barbed wire fence.

I'm ill as a hornet!

I was as mad as a three-legged dog trying to bury a turd on an icy pond.

I'm about to have a duck fit. (Hissy fit, dying duck fit or a hissy fit with a tail on it.)

I'm mad enough to drown puppies.

I'm so mad I could spit!

I'm going to go hunting if it hair-lips the world.

I'm going to skin you alive!

I'm going to jerk you bald!

I'm so mad I could just fall out of my pants.

Mad as a box of frogs.

Mad as a mule chewing on bumblebees.

Madder than a bobcat caught in a piss fire.

Madder than a boiled owl.

Madder than a hornet in a rainstorm.

Madder than a pack of wild dogs on a three legged cat.

Madder than a wet setting hen.

Madder than the snake that married the garden hose!

Meaner than a wet panther.

She's in a horn-tossing mood.

That sticks in your throat like a hair in a biscuit.

Their knickers are in a knot.

You're going to ruffle feathers.

The Weather

Cold enough to freeze the tit off a frog.

Colder than a mother-in-law's kiss.

Colder than a penguin's balls.

It's been hotter than a goat's butt in a pepper patch.

It's been so long since the last rain I had to blow dust out of the rain gauge.

It's cold enough to freeze the balls off a brass monkey.

It's cold enough to freeze the balls off a pool table.

It's colder than a polar bear's toenails.

It's colder than a whore's heart out there.

It's going to be a gully-washer.

It's hotter than a spanked baby's ass.

It's pouring down bullfrogs.

It's raining like a crippled cow peeing on a flat rock. *Jack Berryhill

It's raining pitchforks and plow-handles.

It's so cold I saw a politician with his hands in his own pockets.

It's so hot out here I'm getting swamp ass.

It's colder than a brass toilet seat on the shady side of an iceberg.

It's colder than a witch's titty in a brass bra doing push-ups in the snow.

It's drier than a popcorn fart.

It's gonna be a frog choker.

It's hotter than a goat's ass in a pepper patch.

It's hotter than a hundred acres of burning stumps.

It's hotter than Georgia asphalt.

It's hotter than Hell and half of Georgia.

It's hotter than the Devil's armpit.

It's raining so hard the animals are starting to pair up.

It's so dry the trees are bribing the dogs. (Or whistling for the dogs)

It's so hot I seen a coyote chasing a jackrabbit, and they're both walking.

It's so hot you could sweat 150 pounds of fat off a 75-pound hog.

It's wipe your ass with a snow-cone hot.

Looks like it's coming up a cloud.

So cold we got dogs stuck to fire hydrants all over town.

So hot hens are laying hard-boiled eggs.

The bottom is about to fall out.

Threats

I'll knock you so hard you'll see tomorrow today.

I'll stomp a mud hole in your butt and walk it dry. *Robert RL Pete Ward

Cain't never could.

Don't let your bulldog mouth overload your hummingbird ass.

Don't pee down my back and tell me it's raining!

Don't start none....there won't be none!" *Mandy Graham

Don't let your mouth write a check your butt can't cash.

Don't make me open up a can of whup ass!

Give me the bacon without the sizzle.

Go cork your pistol.

Go peddle your own produce.

Go pound salt up your ass with a wire brush.

Good night nurse!

He didn't know whose weeds he was pissing in.

I didn't just fall off the turnip truck yesterday.

I don't give a hoot 'n holler.

I have three speeds: on, off, and don't push your luck.

I wouldn't give you air if you were in a jug.

I'll be all over you like stink on a skunk.

I'll beat you like a rented mule.

I'll get all over you like white on rice.

I'll jerk a knot in your tail!

I'll kill you and tell God you died.

I'll knock your teeth down your throat and you'll spit 'em

out in single file.

I'll put a knot on your head a calf could suck.
I'll slap some stuff on your head Ajax won't take off.

I'll slap you so hard you'll starve to death before you stop falling.

I'm fixin' ta shut out the lights.

I'm gonna cloud up and make it rain.

I'm gonna cut your tail!

I'm gonna jerk you through a knot.

I'm gonna slap you so hard when you quit rolling' your clothes will be outta style.

I'll hit you so hard your whole family will hurt!

I'll knock a knot on your head so tall you'll have to climb a ladder to comb your hair.

I'll skin you like a Georgia catfish.

I'll smack you so hard your kids will come out behaving.

I'm gonna put a knot in your head the Boy Scouts can't get out.

I'm gonna slap you like a red-headed stepchild.

If you don't stop, I'll tear your arm off and beat you to death with the bloody stump.

It ain't bragging' if you can back it up.

It won't be long now, said the cat when they cut off its tail.

It takes money to ride the train and drink liquor.

Let 'er rip - tater chip.

Me and you are gonna go to fist city.

My God bless your soul, but I have your hide.

My momma didn't drop me off the tater wagon.

Ohhh Hell no! (You should start running.)

Sis on you Pister, you ain't so muckin' fuch!

They better not darken my doorway!
Take your head out of your ass.

Time to paint your butt white and run with the antelope.

Whatever blows your dress up.

When it doubt, knock him out!

You are barking up the wrong tree.

You better give your heart to Jesus, because your butt is

mine.

You don't know doodley squat.

You don't know dip shit from apple butter!

You lie like a dirty cur dog.

You mess with the bull, you get the horns.

You're going to Hell on a scholarship.

You're gonna catch nine shades of Hell.

You're talking like a man with a paper butt.

You lie like a cheap rug. (Or tombstone)

Your promise is like snow in July. *Alicia Hogan

Time

Slap some bacon on biscuit - we're burning daylight. *Brenda Hargrove

Ain't been home since Josie was a calf. *Mike Autry

As long as Pat stayed in the army. (Not long)

Back when men were men and sheep were nervous.

By and by.

Did it in a fever.

Don't spoil Saturday night by counting the time to Monday morning.

Fish or cut bait.

From now until Gabriel blows his horn.

I got up at the butt-crack of dawn.

I will be along directly.

Pulled too green.

Root hog or die.

That won't last two foggy mornings.

The distance to the next milepost depends on the mud in the road.

Thirty years one summer.

Until the cows come home.
We're burning sunlight.

We're trading daylight for dark.

Whenever I start wishing my life away. (Possible answer to: "When am I getting a pony?")

You can't hurry up good times by waiting for them.

You took as long as a month of Sundays.

Touched

As crazy as a betsy bug.

As crazy as an outhouse rat.

Crazier than a dog in a hubcap factory.

Crazier than a shit-house fly.

Crazy as a soup sandwich.

Crazy as a run-over cat.

Crazy as a shot at rat. *Leslie Hobbs

Crazy as a sprayed cockroach.

He's about half a bubble off plumb.

He's two bricks short of a load. Or a beer short of a six-pack. Or a few logs short of a cord. Or a few sandwiches short of a picnic. Or one fry short of a Happy Meal. Or three pickles shy of a quart.

He's lost his vertical hold.

Head full of stump water.

Kangaroos are loose in the top paddock.

Loopy as a cross-eyed cowboy.

Nuttier than a five-pound fruitcake.

Nuttier than a port-a-potty at a peanut festival.

Nuttier than a squirrel turd.

Only got one oar in the water.

She's got a bee in her bonnet.

Slap-assed nutty.

The cheese slid off of that boy's cracker!

The elevator don't go all the way to the top.

The roof ain't nailed tight.

The wheels still turning, but the hamsters died.

You don't have to hang from a tree to be a nut.

Tough

A snake wouldn't bite him without dying.

Could chew up nails and spit out a barbed wire fence.

He goes bear hunting with a switch.

He whips his own ass twice a week.

He's the toughest bastard who ever shit behind shoe leather.

He'd shoot craps with the devil himself.

He's double-backboned.

He's got more guts than you could hang on a fence.

He's the only Hell his mama ever raised.

Like a two dollar steak.

Mean as the alligator when the pond went dry.

Meaner than a skillet full of rattlesnakes.

Scared of nothing but spiders and dry counties.

She raised Hell and stuck a chunk under it.

She would charge Hell with a bucket of ice water.

Tough as nails and twice as sharp.

Tough as stewed skunk.

Tough as whit leather.

Tougher than a one eared alley cat.

Trifling
Don't have a dog in that fight.

He's riding a gravy train on biscuit wheels.

I wasn't sitting on the bedpost.

It's like two mules fighting over a turnip.

Like fleas arguing about who owns the dog.

Six of one - half dozen of another. (Same thing)

That ain't worth the powder to blow it to Hell.

Troublesome

A tough row to hoe.

About as hard as trying to herd chickens.

Between a rock and a hard place.
Easy as pissing up a rope.

Harder to catch than my wife's boyfriend.

He'd complain if he was hung from a new rope.

I'm a stuck duck in a dry pond.

I'm gonna get it done if it harelips every cow in Texas.
(Governor, Pope or President)

It has me by the short and curlies.

It's harder than trying to stick a wet noodle in a wildcat's ass.

Like putting socks on a rooster.

Like snatching shit from a flying goose.

Like trying to bag flies.

Like trying to catch a cat in a whirlwind.

Like trying to herd cats.

Like trying to nail Jell-O to a tree.

Like trying to stack BB's with a catcher's mitt.
Like trying to poke a cat out from under the porch with a rope.

Like trying to shove butter up a wildcat's ass with hot poker.
Like washing a cat.

So heavy it'd take three men and a midget to lift it.

That will separate the sheep from the goats.

Villains
Couldn't fall asleep in a roundhouse.

Crooked as a barrel full of fish hooks.

Crooked as a dog's hind leg.

Crooked as the Brazos.

Full of shit as a Christmas turkey.

Going to blow the gates of Hell wide open when he goes.

He's already got one paw in the chicken coop.

He's trying to cut a fat hog.

He could hide behind a corkscrew.

He knows more ways to take your money than a roomful of lawyers.

He wouldn't know the truth if it slapped him in the face.

He's lower than a snake fart.

He'll put you on the hog train.

He runs with the fox and barks with the hounds.
He's steal the bridle off a night-mare.

He's on a first-name basis with the bottom of the deck.

He's slicker than a boiled onion.

I would not trust him in a shit house with a muzzle.

I wouldn't pee in her ear if her brain was on fire.

I wouldn't trust him any farther than I can throw him.

Meaner than a sack full of rattlesnakes.

More twists than a pretzel factory.

Narrow between the eyes.

One of them will lie and the other one will swear to it.

She's more slippery than a pocketful of pudding.

Slicker than a slop jar.

Slicker than greased owl shit.

So crooked he has to unscrew his britches at night.

So crooked that if he swallowed a nail he'd spit up a corkscrew.

So crooked you can't tell from his tracks if he's coming or going.

Sooner climb a tree to tell a lie than stand on the ground and tell the truth.

Talks out of both sides of his mouth.

The hawk got a job in the chicken yard keeping away the minks.

There are a lot of nooses in his family tree.

Warped like a dogs hind leg.

Well they deserve a front seat in Hell for that. *Andrea Jenea Bobo

You can't polish a turd.

Vittles

Ate that chicken until it was slick as a ribbon.

Barely fit to eat.

Coffee so strong it'll walk into your cup.

Coffee's strong enough to float an iron wedge.

Eating the gospel bird. (Chicken)

Full as a tick on a fat frisky pup.

Good as a cold collard sandwich. (Not good)

Granny cooked enough supper to feed Pharaoh's army. (Cox's or 2nd)

I'm hungry enough to eat a pigtail sandwich. *Mike Autry

If it can't be cooked with bacon grease, it ain't worth making, let alone eating.

If you go away clean you ain't eating it right. (In regards to

BBQ)

It was so good it would have brought tears to a glass eye.

It will make your tongue slap your brains out.

It'll make your liver quiver and your bladder splatter.

My mouth is dry enough to spin cotton.

Put on the dog.

She has on her space panties.

So bad it would snatch the taste right out of your mouth.

So good it'll make your tongue jump out and lick the eyebrows right off your head.

Tastes so good it makes you want to slap your grandma.

That BBQ is tangier than my brother's cutoffs.

That coffee is too thick to drink and too thin to plow.

That ran through me like a dose of salts.

The coffee has been saucered and blowed.

Knock the horns off, wipe its ass, and drag it in. (rare)

Weary

Been chewed up and spit out.

Gone to the Yankees. (Worn out)

He looks like 10 miles of bad road.

I feel like a can of mashed assholes.

I feel like I been eaten by a wolf and shit over a cliff.

I was born tired and I've since suffered a relapse.

One wheel down and the axle dragging.

Petered out.

Plumb tuckered out.

Rode hard and put up wet.

Shot at and missed; shit at and hit.

Slightly burned out, but still smokin'.

Worn to a frazzle.

Well-healed

He buys a new boat when he gets the other one wet.

He has enough money to burn a wet mule.

He's richer than ten inches up a mule's butt.

Living high on the hog.

Richer than Croesus. (The Legendary King of Lydia.)

Shitting in high cotton.

Stiff in the heals.

Walking in tall cotton since Napoleon was in knee pants.

Yankee rich. (Really rich.)

Yes

Ain't that the berries! (That is great!)

Darn Tootin'.

Does a bear shit in the woods?

Does a fat baby fart?

Does a one legged duck swim in a circle?

Does a sack of flour make a mighty big biscuit?
Good Lord willing and the creek don't rise.

I could sit still for that.

I smell what you're stepping in. (or sitting on)

I'd be tickled pink.

Is a ten pound robin fat?

If that ain't a fact, God's a possum.

If you ask kindly, I might could.

Is a frog's ass watertight?

If that ain't right then grits ain't groceries.
Might as well. Can't dance, never could sing, and it's too
wet to plow.

Plumb tickled to death.

Sho 'nuff!

Sure as a cat's got climbing gear.

Straight from the horse's mouth.
That dog will hunt.

You can't beat that with a stick.

Your druthers are my ruthers. (We agree)

You're not just whistling Dixie!

Yonder
A piece down the road.

I had to grease the wagon twice before I hit the main road.

Just a hop skip and a jump. *Judy Noble

Over yonder in the edge of nothing.

They live so far out they have to pipe in sunshine.

Yonder. And Over Yonder. (There, where I would point if momma would let me.)

Book Three: A Sample of Uniquely Southern Terms.

Access road: (service road) "You need to exit the highway to get on the service road."

Addled: (confused) "Grandpa is getting a bit addled."

Adigoglin: (askew) "This room isn't square, it's all adigoglin." (Also catawompus)

Aim to: (going to) "I aim to get my degree in engineering."

Air-Up: (fill up a tire with air) "Please air-up that tire."

All y'all: (used for a large group) "All y'all in the audience are invited."

Alligator pear: (avocado) "Go to the Piggy-Wiggly for an alligator pear."

Ankle beaters: (pants) "Looks like you're expecting high water from the looks of your ankle beaters."

Arkansas toothpick: (large hunting knife) "How sharp is that Arkansas Toothpick?"

Badmouth: (insult) "Don't badmouth your teacher."

146

Balls to the walls: (going all out) "We were going balls to the wall when Billy fell off his skis."

Banquet: (sidewalk in southern LA and MS) "Don't ride your bike on the banquet"

Bifold: (billfold or wallet) "Hey, that Yankee took my bi-fold."

Bless your heart: (concern or contempt). At the end of a phrase such as: "She likes her cocktails - bless her heart." - the phrase conveys a level of concern. On the other hand, if "Bless your heart" follows a statement by another person it is often meant to be in contempt. For example if someone said to a Southerner: "I don't understand the fuss about college football." The Southerner will likely respond with: "Why, bless your heart." Translated to Yankee this would mean: "You are a freaking idiot."

Boggin': (off-roading) "The jeep is clean, let's go boggin'!

Bread Basket: (stomach) "She hit him right in the bread-basket."

Buggy: (shopping cart) "There were no buggies at the Piggly Wiggly."

Carry: (take) "Please carry me to Walmart."

Carry on: (To make a scene foolishly) "Missy, what are you carrying on about?"

Cattywampus: (askew) "That house is all cattywampus since the flood."

Clicker: (remote control) "If I could find the clicker we could watch 60-minutes."

Chief Cook and Bottle Washer: (jack of all trades) "I'm the CEO, Chief Cook and Bottle Washer."

Chin musician: (chatty) "That man drones away like a chin musician."

Chugged full: (full and over-flowing) "That cooler is chugged full of catfish."

Chunk: (throw) "I can chunk a football 50 yards."

Coke: (soda) "What kind of Coke do you want in your bourbon, Sprite or Ginger?"

Conniption: (angry) "Momma will have a conniption if I'm late."

Conniption fit: (angry) "A threat level above "conniption."

Contrary: (disagreeable) "Why must you be so contrary when we're picking a restaurant?"

Cooler-aider: (refrigerator) "Make sure you put the coke in the cooler-aider."

148

Crawfishin' or Crawdadin': (going back on your word). "He won't crawdad on the deal, we shook on it."

Crik: (stream or brook) "What lake does this crik empty into?"

Darn near: (almost) "That fish darn near took my bait."

Dingle: (penis) "Stop playing with your dingle."

Dirt nap: (death) "I'm not ready for the flowers and dirt nap yet."

Do go on: (Please stop, you must be joking) "You've seen someone floss their teeth at dinner? Please do go on"

Do what?: (Don't ask again!) Question: "Can I wear tennis shoes to the prom?" Answer: "Do what?"

Egg-on: (antagonize) "Don't egg-on your sister."

Feisty: (frisky) "Whiskey makes my girlfriend feisty."

Figure: (to think) "I didn't figure on finding good BBQ in New York, and I didn't."

Fit to be tied: (angry) "After she stood me up, I was fit to be tied."

Fixin' ta: (about to do something) "I'm fixin' ta carry momma to Piggly Wiggly."

Flap-Doodle! (dammit!) "Flap-doodle, the Bulldogs lost."

Foolin' round: (making mischief) "You kid stop that foolin' around."

Frog strangler: (heavy rain) "Last week the damn almost breached in that frog strangler."

Fur piece: (long distance) "Just about anywhere is a fur piece from here."

Gator mouth: (bad teeth) "Someone take that gator mouth to find a dentist!"

Gets it honestly: (hereditary) "Her daddy was a Hell raiser, so she comes by it honestly."

Gimme sugar: (give me a kiss) "Give grandma some sugar."

Got a good notion: (idea) "I have a good notion to play golf."

Grocery feet: (very dirty feet) "You better not bring grocery feet into this house."

Gully washer: (a heavy rain) "That gully washer broke my tomato plants."

Gussied up: (dressed up) "Momma is all gussied up for the party."

Haint: (ghost) "I'm going to the party dressed as a haint."

Hankering (a desire) "I have a hankerin' for some pecan pie."

Heap: (a lot of something) "You're in a heap of trouble now."

Hear tell: (I've heard, or also tell me more) "I hear tell that the new Walmart has sushi and bait."

High tail it: (leave rapidly) "We better high tail it before your daddy sees this."

Hissy fit: (angry) "I thought momma was going to have a hissy fit over the spilled milk."

Hitch: (marry) "Rhett ain't never getting hitched to Scarlet again."

Hold your water: (wait) "Just hold your water, we're fixin' to go."

Honky tonk: (country bar) "That new honty tonk is way out in the sticks."

Horse sense: (common sense) "That lady has good horse sense in running that business."

House shoes: (bedroom slippers) "I taught my dog to fetch my house shoes."

Howdy: ("Hi" mostly in Texas) "Howdy folks, welcome to DFW."

Hunkey dorey: (doing good) "I'm just hunkey dorey!"

Hush puppies: (deep fried cornbread) "We're having hush puppies and a mess of fish for dinner."

Hush your mouth: (quiet) "Hush your mouth, I only drink socially."

I aim to: (I plan to) "I aim to get my degree in engineering."

I can't know: (don't know and don't want to.) "You hear about the neighbors? Answer: I can't know it."

I swannie: (I swear) "I swannie, that kid is giving me gray hairs."

Idjit: (idiot) "She's such an idjit about men."

It ain't fittin': (It's not right)"It ain't fittin' that they sent him on a snipe hunt twice."

It makes no never mind: (it's of no consequence.) "Dagnabbit! I forgot the milk! Response: "It makes no never mind, we still have some."

Knee babies: (toddlers) "Knee babies are called rug rats up north."

Lagniappe: (a little something extra) "That little chocolate on your pillow is a lagniappe."

Larking: (for pleasure) "We're just larking around town."

Lawdy: (good Lord) "Lawdy, my feet are sore."

Laying out: (out all night drinking) "After homecoming we laid out all night."

Lead pill: (bullet) "Nothing wrong with him a lead pill can't fix."

Liable to: (I might just) "I'm liable to dance if properly motivated."

Lick and a promise: (hope) "The roof is fixed with a lick and a promise."

Lickered up: (liquored up-drunk) "We're all lickered up after the Iron Bowl."

Lickety split: (quickly) "After the dance, we go out of there lickety split."

Like to: (nearly) "I was so embarrassed I liked to died."

Lunch puppy: (someone who enjoys eating) "Don't set the cornbread next to Tim, he's a real lunch puppy."

Mash: (to push) "Mash the doorbell please."

Mater: (tomato) "I'd like a mater sandwich with mayonnaise please."

Mending fences: (to make up with someone) "Those two in the corner are mending fences, let them be."

Mess: (several helpings of food) "We're cooking up a mess of peas."

Mind to: (thinking about) "I have a mind to wash the dog."

Nearabout: (almost) "'I nearabout fell off the coach when phone rang."

Neutral ground: (the median strip of a highway) "Look out for broken glass on the neutral ground."

No 'count: (person of low regard) "That man was no 'count since we were kids."

Off kilter: (not right, out of whack.) "That kid is a little off kilter."

Ornery: (irritable) "Daddy is ornery since Auburn beat us."

Out of kilter: (out of sorts) "That tire is out of kilter."

Over Yonder. (Just over there.) "The baggage claim is just over yonder."

Ownliest: (single) "You are my ownliest love, Scarlet."

Peanut hog: (obese) "The peanut hogs are always at the buffet."

People: (relatives) "We're spending Christmas with daddy's people."

Persnickety: (fussy) "Don't be so persnickety about your guest list."

Pert' near. (Close to) "Pert' near time to go home."

Pick at: (peck) "Don't pick at your dinner, eat it."

Piddlin': (small) "My bonus was just piddlin' this year."

Piece goods: (bolts of fabric) "Momma bought some piece goods for my new dress."

Pipe down: (quiet) "You kids pipe down to a low roar!"

Plague take: (a curse) "Plague take that dog for getting into the trash."

Play pretty: (toys) "Pick up your play-pretties or I'm keeping them."

Playin' possum: (pretending to be asleep) "You're not asleep, you're playin' possum."

Plike: (play-like or pretend) "Let's plike I'm a doctor and you're a patient."

Plumb: (totally) "I am plumb wore out from dancing."

Po'Boy: (sub sandwich) "Oyster po-boys are just about the

finest thing you can put in your mouth."

Pocketbook: (purse) "Hey, that Yankee took my pocketbook."

Pray tell: (Not believing someone) "Your sister threw a baseball through the window - pray tell?"

Privy: (outhouse) "Which way to the privy?"

Puny: (small) "That boy sure is puny."

Purdy: (pretty) "You smell purdy."

Put up: (canning produce) "We're putting up peaches this weekend."

Rag-baby: (doll) "Please pick up your ragdoll."

Reckon: (to figure) "I reckon that we have two hours of daylight left."

Right at it: (meaning almost) "Is it time to go to the party?" Answer: "Right at it!"

Right quick: (do it now!) "Pour me another oyster shooter right quick?"

Rile: (anger) "Don't rile your sister."

Shine: (attraction) "Your brother has taken a shine to my sister."

Show: (movies) "Hey, what's playing at the show this week?"

Skank: (low-class) "That girl he's dating ain't nothing but a skank."

Skedaddle: (leave quickly) "We better skedaddle back home for dinner."

Slew-footed: (pigeon toed) "No wonder that horse is slow, it's slew footed."

Snake-bit: (unlucky) "I am just snake-bit so you won't see me at the casino."

Snipe huntin': (fool's errand) "Looking for a blue squirrel is just snipe hunting."

Snug as a bug: (cozy) "This blanket leaves me snug as a bug."

Stomping grounds: (place of youth) "Memphis is my old stomping grounds."

Stove up: (cramped or sore) "I'm all stove up after playing football with the youngins'"

Sugar: (kiss) "Come here and give me some sugar."

Sweeper: (vacuum) "Please don't run the sweeper during football season."

Tacky: (shameful) "Wearing tennis shoes with a tuxedo is just tacky."

Tadlaripin: (delicious) "Those greens are tadlaripin."

Teched: ("touched", crazy) "Jed is teched in the head."

Testosterone poisoning: (too many men) "The booster club is suffering from testosterone poisoning."

Tickled: (to laugh) "That joke about the preacher tickled me."

Tore up: (drunk or upset) "I am tore up from bloody marys."

Tote: (carry) "May I tote your bags?"

Tow head: (blond) "When he was a little, he was a tow head."

Trade: (occupation) "I'm thinking about writing as a trade."

Trotline: (long line fishing) "We caught this mess of fish on the trotline."

Tuckered out: (exhausted) "I am tuckered out from watching football."

Tump: (turn over) "Tump over that ice cooler please."

Unbeknownst: (unknown) "Unbeknownst to me, the keg

went dry at the BBQ."

Uppity: (conceited) "Don't be uppity with me young lady."

Varmint: (pest) "We have some varmints in the garden."

Vittles: (victuals) "What vittles are we having for supper?"

Washateria: (laundromat) "Can you get some quarters for the washateria."

Weenie: (hotdog) "Let cook some weenies on the campfire."

What in Sam Hill: (surprise) "What in Sam Hill happened to my penny loafers?"

Whup: (to beat up) "Mow the yard or I'm gonna whup your behind."

Y'all: (pronounced like "yol") "How y'all doin'?

Yestiddy: (yesterday) "That project was due yestiddy."

Yonder: (just over there) "It's just over yonder. No, I won't point to it and you can't get there from here. Best just to come back from whence you came"

Youngin': (child) "What is that youngin' up to now!"

Book Four: Contributors and Some of Their Favorite Sayings.

Kay Humphreys Abernathy: "Not much punkin." , "If it ain't bedbugs it's piss ants." and "no so forty."

Carol Jones Adair: "Hasn't got enough sense to pour piss out of a boot!", and "slow as Christmas!"

Jimmy D Adams: "That's as slick as a peeled onion."

Thelma Adams: "Don't put those elbows on the table." My grandma would send you from the table.

Kitty Crocker Aldridge: "Six of one, half a dozen of the other."

Barry Aluisa: "plumb out."

Brenda Parker Anderson: Daddy always said: "Time to go lay the ole frame down."

Mike Autry: "Ain't been home since Josie was a calf." and "I'm hungry enough to eat a pig tail sammich."

Charles Avent: "Well, I'll be a suck-egg mule!" and. "Ding-DANG it!" and "Buck Nekkid".

Angela Stamson Baker: "Oh for pity's sake!"

Mary Parker Ballou: "I ain't had so much fun since the hogs ate my little brother!"

Karen Crockett Barmer: My dad would say "she ain't purdy none, she'd make a freight train take a dirt road."

Michael Barnes: "More than carter has liver pills."

Dinah Bates: "You can get happy in the same shoes you got mad in!!!"

Don Beasley: "Happy as a possum in a persimmon tree."

Beth Belcher: "Stop pooting around", "Good night nurse!"

Diane Belluso: "y'all come back now."

Cammie Beckwith Bennett: "Anything with a beak and a wing is a beautiful thing."

Sharon Cain Bentz: "Well Dag Nabbit!"

Patti Bernier: "Not reading all but I say "over yonder" a lot!"

Kay Cartwright Berry: "It'll never be noticed on a galloping horse."

Jack Berryhill: "Raining like a crippled cow peeing on a flat rock."

John Bethea: "You preaching to the choir."

Mary Frances Bingham-Mcgee: my mom would say she, "Hope someone to do the dishes" instead of she "helped" someone.

Kathleen Gallagher Bishop: When Dad didn't like us to be around certain wild teens he would say, :"You mess with sh*t, you get it on you."

Ed Blackburn: "Hurry up don't dilly-daddy."

Riva Pittman Blair: "If if's and buts were candies and nuts everyday would be Christmas."

Sherry Haynes Blake: "ohh Hell to the naw."

Andrea Jenea Bobo: "You'd worry the horns off a billy goat." and "That kid could wreck a steel ball."

Jeanette Facello Boling: "Your daddy wasn't a glass maker."

Mike Bostic: "Don`t squat down with your spurs on."

Vickie J Boulton: "Who'll know the difference in a hundred years?" My grandmother's favorite.

Shannon Sonricker Bower: "Losing my religion.", "Lipstick on a pig." and "You can go to Hell for lying as fast as you can for stealing."

Janice Box-Franklin: One of mine is "Oh lord help····get my brandy···I am about to have the vapors."

Jimmy Bozeman: "He/She can worry the horns off a billygoat."

Marla Gann Bracey: "Holler if you need me."

Rebecca Bradley: "Crazy as a Betsy bug."

Evelyn Osbourne Bradshaw: "If it's not bedbugs, it's piss ants!"

Cynthia Shellabarger Brashier: "Knock about clothes" referring to wearing clothes to work or play in opposed to dressing up to go out.

Ramona Breazeale: "fair to middling", So good makes you want to slap your mama."

Derek Brewer: "I'd rather sandpaper a bobcat's ass in a phone booth."

Doris Wise Britt: My mother never cooked in a 'pot'...she called them a 'steer'.

Connie Browder: "To beat ninety."

Bettie Johnston Bryant: "Don't come running to me if you fall out of that tree and break your leg."

Sheila Humphreys Bryant: "I'm sicken tried."

Susan Stafford Buck: "You can't fool God and you can't fool me!"

Cindy Jackson Buckley: "If a frog had wings, it wouldn't bump its butt when it hops."

Jay Buse: "His cheese has done slid off his cracker."

Carol Byrnes: "Poke me with a fork, I'm done." I say "Full as a tick on a hound-dog's ear."

Kimbra Callahan: "Want in one hand and sh** in the other and see which one fills up the fastest."

Vicki Campbell-Cohn: "Fixing to."

Carol Cannon: "Oh Lord, I know so many Southern-isms I don't know where to start - opps, I believe that was one right there"

Dawn Cannon: "The bottom is about to fall out"

Jeanann Rodgers Caraway: Gonnna eat me a pack of NABS, and drink a COKE (with a pack of peanuts in it)!

Mark Caraway: "He thinks he's in high cotton."

Jackie Card: "Caint win fer losin`!"

Carol Atkinson Carlson: "Stop that and act like a lady", " Dag nab it!", "God willin' an' the crick don't rise."

Johnny Carroll: my Uncle Bizer, use to say to me," your butt will be glad when your head dies."

Bill Carson: "Give me a swig" and you are crying and trying to stop my mom would say, "Dry it up!"

Edith Carson: "Plum outta town and nelly outta the country."

Connie Carter: "You can get glad in the same breaches you got mad in."

Jeana Myers Cassis: "Thing a ma jig."

Tracey Dukes Castillo: "That one over there thinks he's diamond Jim.".

David Chamberlain: "Nervous as a cat in a room full o' rockin' chairs."

James Chandler: "Boy you make a better wall than window."

Tim Chiles: "Stop that crying or I'll give you something to cry about."

Debbie Ladd Chisolm: "I'm gonna turn you over my checkity apron."

Rene Claunch: " I'm so broke I can't pay attention····well, I'll be dipped···hard row to hoe···it the good lord is willing and the creeks don't rise."

Guy Gloria Cofer: "She can't help it." and "Happy as a tick on a dog."

Keith Cole: "I am a fixin' to." and "Bless their heart."

Jane Dawson Coley: "I'm gonna snatch you bald if you do that again!"

Michael Collins: "Bless their li'l Hearts."

Eleana Andrews Cooley: Just got thru puttin' on the dog for Christmas dinner.

Kenny Cooper: "It's raining like a cow pissing on a flat rock!"

JoeAnn Cordell: "You can't make a silk purse out of a sows ear."

Nancy Murphy Covington: "Homegrown ugly!"

Christi Jewel Melton Cox: "I'll give u a Yankee dime if u go" .... Whatever she wanted u to do!

Anne J. Creekmore: "That's like herding cats."

Susan McGreger Crisler: "Yesterdeaving" for yesterday evening.

Betty Cropper: "Y'all come back to see us now."

Dorothy Gibson Cruthirds: "Full as tick!"

Philip Cruzen: "The fella has a much business with (fill in the blank) as a hog has with a side saddle."

Kathy Hampton Culver: I always liked, "How's your Mom n

'em?"

Thomas Cumberland: "Don't carry a knife to a gun fight."

Renee Daniels: "That was so good it'll make you slap yo mama."

Mary Helen Yearout Darden: "Cut the light off." , "Once in a blue moon." and "Tighter than bark on a tree."

Paula Taylor Davidson: "Give you a buzz.". "Uglier than a mud fence dobbed with lizards."

Laura Davidson: "Art" as is in, "You art not act like that in public." and "Dog barn it! I'm maddern' a nest o hornets!"

Stephanie C. Davis: "Dumb as dirt.", "I shore hate it!"

Kim Davis: "Now y'all know God don't like ugly so be nice!"

Mark Davis: "Well I swanny!" and "You'd put up a sign post and then argue with it."

Robert Davis: "Now your putting some bacon in the skillet", "So broke we can't pay attention", "Can't make chicken salad outta chicken sh!t."

Diane Vaccaro Davison: "It's hotter than······Hades!" and "Loved my Momma 'to pieces'."

Alan Dearman: "His eyes were so crossed, he could keep one eye on the snake and look for a stick to kill him with the other eye·"

Harry Dedmon: "We will be there if the creek don't rise and the horses don't break the trace chains·"

Susie Dent: "As scarce as hen's teeth·"

Jennifer Dickson: "Slap the stew out of you!"

Terri Walters Dishon: "fair to middling"

Fred Doane: Are you busy?····Response, "My @$$ is on fire and my hair is catchin'·"

Don Drane: "This is gonna hurt me more than it will you·"

Sherry Eaton: "Don't take any wooden nickels·"

Lorella Edmondson: "He's polite as a bag of chips"

Sonia Elfeki: "As nervous as a long tailed cat in a room full of rocking chairs·"

Jimmy Ellis: "If you play Guitar·"

Anita C Estep: "I swonee!" Grandmother wouldn't say, "I swear·"

Eva Evans: "I'm fixing to"····in the place of I'm going to····"

Patrick Evans: "More problems than Carter's got liver pills·"

Ann Fassetta: "Y'all come back now·"

Debbie McAdams Faught: "Drunk as a piss ant."

Debbie Dobbs Fields: "Pretty is as pretty does."

Elizabeth Vest Figueroa: "BRING IT DOWN TO A ROAR"

Foster C. FitzHugh: "Looks like the south end of a
northbound jackass."

Beverly Mimi Caldwell Fletcher: "If you get a whippin at
school you get a whippin at home."

Donna Hearn Flint: "I'm going to slap you into next week."

Aimee Merritt Floyd: "Raining cats n dogs."

Karen Pulfer Focht: "Can you carry me to the store?" and
"She's a mess.", "What church do you belong to?"

Lisa Marie Force: "I'm fixin to do that."

Ginger Henley Ford: "Lord, have mercy.", my friend would
say. "well, flea ants". My aunt,"good lack uh day".

Laura Penna Ford: "Dad gum it." and "I'll be dog gone."

Tom Ford: "Awwwww shucks.","Dad burn it.","Gee
whilikers.", "I don't spect I will.", "I speck so."

Shawna Fore: "Bless her heart."

Marian Dulaney Fortner: "Don't worry about the mule going
blind, just load the wagon!"

Marcy Foster: "You need to straighten up and fly right!!! Or you will go to Hell in a wheel barrow."

Laura McWilliams Fox: "We are going to have a come to Jesus meeting." and "I am going to have a come apart."

Ruby Oliver French: "Well I swannie !"

David Gaddie: "Fools' names and fools' faces always appear in public places."

Mandy Gann: "I'm as tired as a poot in a whirlwind."

Rusty Gardner: "You lookin at me like cow lookin at a new gate."

Wanda Gail Gardner: What not now? (what's happening?) "You make a better door than a window" (move out of my line of vision).

Katie Allen Gholson: "I'm so hungry I could eat the rear end out of a rag doll." and "Strung out like goats."

Stacey Moses Gibson: "Dumber than a box of Rocks!" and "Need to change the oil in them Clothes."

Tammy Douris Goins: "Your ass is grass and I am the lawnmower."

Robert Gonzales: "You are barkin up the wrong tree."

Carolyn Graham: "It'll all come out wash day."

Mandy Graham: "Don't start none- there won't be none·····!"

John Gray: "John Brown it!" and "That's slicker than owl poop·"

Lynn Grier: "Bless your heart·"

Leanne Grilli: "Bless her/his heart·"

Beth Guthrie: "A whistlin' girl and a crowin' hen, always come to a no good end·"

Jeri Hale: "You going to the movies? Then quit picking your seat· (When someone was pulling at their pants)

Sherree Aeschliman Hamby: "Useless as a screen door on a submarine·"

Laura Hames: my Granny would say, "dreckly" which meant "directly"·

Linda Hammack: "Bless your heart!!"

Chasity N Michael Harbour: "It's so hot out here I'm getting swamp ass·"

Brenda Hargrove: "Slap some bacon on biscuit, we're burning daylight·"

Rita Langley Moran Harris: "She looks like death sitting on tombstones hatching haints·"

Ann Clark Harris: "Faster(or quicker) than Sherman going thru Georgia!"

Mona Davis Harris: "You can just get glad in the same shoes you got mad in." and ".Cooking a mess of greens."

Fran Hart: "Get outside and play and don't y'all come back in here til dark!"

Harry Harwell: "Going through life with blinders on." and "Dead as a door nail." and " Like catchin fish in a barrel."

Sane Hatter: "I look like ten miles of bad road!"

Christi Whitsell Hawkins: "I'm so hongry (hungry) I could eat a horse."

Eddy Hays: "I brought you into this world I'll take you out."

Vicky Heathcock: "Katy bar the door!"

Gayle Heaton: "Don't be ugly to your sister." and "Eat like the govenor." (Meaning:Elbows off the table, Miss Gov. had one arm.)

Tim B. Heaton: "This ain't fit to eat."

Lynn Hester: "Dem dar folkes over dunder."

Pam Hill: "Bless his heart he's a Yankee and don't know no better."

MelissanRandy Hilton: When people call "parking spots" ...."sparking spots."

Leslie Hobbs: "Crazy as a shot rat."

Alicia Hogan: "Your promise is like snow in July"

Montie Holbrook: "Gosh darn it."

Phyllis Holder: "Shut that door·······were you raised in a barn???"

Beverly Cole Hooker: "It "tumped" over."

Jennifer Horn: "Don't get your piss hot, it will burn your kidneys out!"

Sheri Houart: "What are you doing? Answer:pickin up paw-paws & puttin 'um in a basket or just messin & gobbin."

Becca Howell: "Can you carry me up to the store? There's enough food for Cox's Army!"

Kathy Hurley: "That dog won't hunt!!!"

Demitra Hutchison: " Well, I'll be John Brown!!!"

Kay Hutto: "I haven't seen y'all in coons ages."

Nelson Ingram: "Tight as Dick's hat band!"

Anna Irwin: "You are giving me the "wooly bullies""·

James Oliver Cox IV: "Bless your heart.", "I'm fixing too."

Dana Andrews Ivy: "Bless her/his heart", "Drunker than Cooter Brown"

Gina Koury Jackson: "Bless your heart."

Jonathan Jamerson: "Nuttier than a squirrel turd."

Jaymie Wakeland Jarman: "Be sweet" when going to school or church.

Joyce Smith Jernigan: "Bless their heart.", and "You made this bed, you can sleep in it."

Jimmy Dale Johnson: "So dumb they couldn't herd ducks to water in front of a pond."

Bobby Johnson: "That dog don't hunt here!"

Liz Johnson: "Give us some sugar." and "Looked like he/she just stepped out of a band box."

Terry Jo Jones: "To see a man about a dog"

Nikita Jones: "A dog named Bog. Give him something once, he'll want it all."

Forrest Joyner: "Couldn't carry a tune in a bucket." and "Couldn't pour piss out of a boot with directions on the heel."

Toni Smith Justice: "I will be on you like white on rice, happier than a pig in slop, colder than a well diggers butt in China"

Ruthie Snyder Kaser: "Finer than frog hair split two ways." and "Full as a tick on a fat frisky pup".

Ron Kattawar: "I'll need a Kroger sack to hold all of that."

Susan Keller: "I swannie!", "make groceries."

Shea Sparks Kelley: "I'm fixin to crank the car."

Anthony Kelley: "I'm gonna pull out a can of whoop ass on you."

Dawn Freeman Kidd: "Couple a miles as a crow flies."

Steven Killebrew: "Knee-slapping funny."

Susan McNally Killian: "You make my butt wanna dip snuff."

Ken Kirby: "Well I ain't never!"

Donnie Kisner: "Is a bullfrog waterproof?"

Terri Richards Knight: "I'll be there directly", "Its gonna take a rusty corncob to get this dirt off you."

Dianne Read Lancaster: "Well, if that don't take the rag off the bush!"

Rhonda Murrah Landrum: "I'll fix your little red wagon."

Patricia Blaylock Langford: My mother still says: "Now be sweet" or "That's not pretty".

Gayle Langford: "It's a gully washer."

Erick Lashley: "If a snapping turtle bites you it wont let go til it thunders."

Peggie Leaptrott: "I'll slap you into the middle of next week."

Patricia Jones Lee: "He/She is older than dirt!!!"

Jim Leggett: my dad to reckless and Drunk drivers, "Drive on Hell ain't half full."

Gigi Goss Lewis: "Sop that gravy with that biscuit boy, don't you go ta wastin' food."

Nanacita Lewis: "It flew all over me", "She was all over me like an ugly dress."

Rhonda Lindsay: My dad would say, "going to the Jiffy Rip"when going to a 7-11 or magic mart

Gil Little: "Killed it dead"

Joy Hardy Locke: "Be particular now, ya hear!"

Jimmy Long: "I'm 'fixing to send you one."

Donna Hannah Looney: "I don't know if I should wind my

a$$ or wipe my clock."""

Phylis Walker Lovell: My mother always told me, "A Lady only chews gum in the privacy of her boudoir. "

Alice Lurker: When something is delicious, it's "tadlaripin"

Jeanette Thompson Maddox: "That swing set's gonna tump over!"

Ginny Hawks Malfa: "Lord have mercy."

Laura Marsh: "Fixin' ta." The first time I left the south I had no idea that the rest of the world did not say that.

Clara Delk Martin: "My daddy called meringue "calf slobber.""

Priscilla May: "It's seems to me that you are itchin' for a switchin'!"

Adele McCall: "The gophers are nibbling at his toes."
(Someone close to death)

Beverly A McCammon: "All stoved up."

Tarrell Mac McCrory: "He is a few boles shy of a full bale."

David McDaniel: "Well for Pete's sake !!" Never knew who "Pete" was.

Ruth Hall McFall: "Durn it.", "Eatin high on the hog.",

177

"Got a bee in her bonnet." and "Got a stitch in my side."

Lisa McGee: "That's your red wagon to pull."

Mike McGee: "I think I'll go out among the dry cattle"- don't know what it means but my Dad use to say it.

Mariechen Woodworth McGruder: Granny use to tell us, "just sit there and sip your tea" or "I'm just sippin' my tea." meant minding my own business.

Polly Anne McMath McKaskle: "My grandfather used to tell me I was the sweetest thing this side of Mobile."

Betty Wynne Mckinley: "If you don t stop that I am going to hit you with a shelaylee."

Don McMinn: "Come over here and hug my neck!" My Aunt Virginia use to say that to me every time she saw me.

Charles Edwin McNabb: "Mind your manners," and "You look like the north end of a south bound mule."

Jeanette Bobo Mcneil: "Over yonder."

Leeann M. McNinch: I never knew what "lolly gagging" was but was accused of it.

Mike McOwen: "This is more fun than Sunday school " or "Sunday on the farm."

Kay McPherson: "He ain't worth the wagon he rode in on."

and "too many cooks and not enough injuns"

Suzanne Melton: "Bless your heart."

Melinda Milam: "A hard rain is a 'frog strangler'"

Donna Jo Dillard Miles: "Bless her heart, she is dumber than dirt."

Bernice W. Miller: "Over yonder."

Ken Miller: "She was uglier than a mud fence."

Shirley Stewart Millican: "If the Lord is willing, and the creek don't rise" and "You might oughta."

MaryAnn Millican: "that cotton picking dog just ----"

Lori Deen Mitchell: "Can't. Never could."

Tom Moak: "Faster than an old woman catchin a cold."

Thomas Tommy Morgan: "Raining so hard it sounds like a cow peeing on a flat rock."

Bob Morgan: My favorite from my dad, James L. Morgan, "Can't never could do nothing."

Chris Morgan: "Colder'n blue flugens!"

Mary Morris: "Its cold as a well diggers ass in January." and "Hotter than a six-shooter."

Mavis Morton: "Slicker than deer guts on a door knob."

Jo Angela Moses: "It's raining cats, and dogs!"

Joy Mounce: "He stinks to high heaven!", "Heavens to Betsy!" and "You're from my neck of the woods."

Charlie Musselwhite: "I'll whip ya 'till your nose ropes like okra and yo' butt smells like burnt boot."

Bob Nelson: "It's fixing to come up a cloud." and "That boy's the nearest nothin'."

Johnnie Hughes Netherland: "He doesn't have a pot to piss in or a window to pour it out of."

Gary Nevin: "Crazy as a run over dog." and "Thanks MR GRADY."

Stan Nichols: "Lost as a goose in a hail storm." and "I don't know whether to pee or wind my watch."

Judy Noble: "You make your bed, you lay in it." (My dad's favorite!) and "Denial ain't just a river in Egypt."

Margie Blanchard O'Neal: "Bless her heart."

Heather Boren Oakes: "It's hotter than 15 Hells outside.", "Heck Fire and dang nations." and "Taint seen y'all (yew) since hector was a pup"

Mary Odom: "I'm gonna getchew.", "Make you wanna slap

yo momma, its so good." and "Yall quit it."

Cindie Orange: "Bless his little heart."

Mark Overby: "Does bout as much good as windshield wipers on a ducks butt."

Tom Owens: when I worked delivering groceries my boss would tell me, "Turn your around so I will think you are coming back."

Brenda Pafford: "Throw it up to the wind and let the dust settle it."

Rosalie Palazzolo: "Hows ur mama and them?"

LaTonya Davis Parham: "It's better to be pissed off then pissed on."

Joseph Parker: "I'm gonna dust your britches."

Lisa Moore Parkes: One of my mother's favorites·· "I don't give a rat's ass!" "Don't that beat all"· "Lordy mercy."

Randy Partridge: "Like cows at the feed trough."

Toni Hartley Suzore Patrick: "Bass ackwards", "You ain't dry behind the ears", "he ain't worth a plug nickel", "you must think I am Ned in the 1st reader", "you got 2 ears and 1 mouth what does that tell ya!"

Michael Patterson: "Big-O" as in "That shore is a big-o

truck."

Pat Patterson: "Get a -holt of yourself!"

Sheri May Pecukonis: "I believe I am going to go get in the hay!"

Mike Pendergrass: "Day late and a dollar Short."

Alexandria Perel: "Do what?", "Puny." "Know what I'm sayin?"

Traci Barnhill Perkins: "Tastes so good, make you wanna smack your mama!"

Eddie Perkins: "With a hole in the toe."

Todd B. Pigott: "Now isn't that about as dumb as a bag of hammers."

Chuck Pigue: "Go over yonder and sit your butt down; I'm a fixin to get me a switch."

Malcolm Platt: "Happier'n a puppy with two peckers."

Mike Polsky: "Fold it 7 times and put it where the sun don't shine." and "Yard eggs."

Lynn Poor: "Don't get your panties in a wad!" Her skirt's "butt sprung." and "That's where the Yankee shot you. (Your navel)

Robin Potter: "Shit fire and save matches."

ChristyAnn Pounders: "I'm gonna stomp a mud hole in you and walk it dry!"

Memphis Bluesman Preston: "You just keep living!"

Victoria Prevost: "As scared as a long tail cat in a room full of rockers."

Gail Price: "Are you in your shimmy tail?", "Better than a poke in the eye with a short stick.", "Help me I'm hung! (Stuck)"

Sandra Carpenter Putz: "God don't like ugly." (Meaning be nice).

Kara R: "Haven't seen you in a minute."

Robert Ramsey: "That dog will hunt! Tighter than Dick's hatband!"

Pam Frye Reed: "Well, I swanee."

Samantha Reed: "If I'd known you was a coming I'd known what to do I'd raised both hands and I'd wove at you."

Betty Regan: "fixin' to."

Shuyler Chuck Reid: "Running like he stole something!"

Jim Reid: "He's got a face that would make a freight train

take a dirt road!"

Dru Reynolds: "Jumping around like piss ants on a hot griddle."

Sandy White Rhodes: "Bless her heart!" and "I am fixing to go."

Jim Rhodes: "Doesn't know craps from Crisco." and "Bless his/her little heart."

Debbie Richerson: "I'll break you down like a shotgun!"

Vicki Riddle: "He's tighter than Dick's hatband."

Stephen Risher: "Hey y'all, watch this!" [famous last words]

Robbie Robbins: "He couldn't hit a bull in the butt with a bass fiddle!"

Cathy J. Roberts: "Wild as March hair!"

Gloria Goode Roberts: Mother would say, "Want in one hand – spit in the other hand and see which one fills up the fastest".

Mike Robertson: "She was from Plum Nelly." Plum outta the country and nelly outta the world! (Thanks, for that one, Uncle Buford.)

Chuck Rodgers: "He's as messed up as a soup sandwich."

Wayne Rolin: "She talked to me like I was a yard dog."

Danny Rooker: "Boy you ain't skint right." and "I'll give you a Yankee dime."

Jaime Crosby Ross: "Its like Heading cats.", "Well I'll be."

Tonya Mallette Rowland: "I brought u in this world I can take you out."

Tommy Russell: "Dummer than the leading edge on a basketball."

Marilyn Upchurch Rutledge: "Shor as snuff."

Kathy Hilliard Sanders: "Well Hell fire and shi& matches," and "I'm fixin to put some nickel knots on your head."

Susannah McCafferty Sanders: "Looks like something the cat drug home and the kittens wouldn't eat!"

David Sappington: Always a favorite word- "catawampus" meaning anything out of order.

Tommy Sayers: "I'm fixing to go downtown."

Susie Schell: "Don't talk back."

Kenneth Schildt: "Well, don't that take the rag off of the the bush?"

Cathy Wyatt Schroeder: "It ain't fittin'."

Brenda Lambert Scott: "Put your shoes on Susie and don't you take them off!" -it was an old song my dad would sing to us.

Gene Scott: "Might don't pick no cotton!"

Dee Sebree: Only in the south can you say, "Well I declare" followed by no declaration.

Connie Beckwith Self: "You aint right.", "That aint right."and "You wrong for that."

Chris McDavid Selph: "I could ride to town on that lip!" (Pouting)

Bill Shaeffer: "Well I ain't never."

Peggy Landrum Shanks: "Git over yonder!

Nan Sherlin: "She was so slappass ugly, I 'bout fell out!"

Larry Shields: "Did you everrrr···?"

Fay Holloway Shiers: "I'm gonna pop you bald headed."

Alan Shows: "Dat ain't right."

Diamond Sibley: "I'm out of pocket today"

Debbie Nicholson Sims: "For land's sakes!" and "Grinnin' like a mule eatin' paste,"

Carolyn Slay-Jones: My great grandmother would say, "Make

haste there ain't no coming back."

Sarah Wallace Smith: "Best thing since sliced bread."

Angela Smith: "There's a dead cat on the line."

Charles Smith: "Gotta alligator mouth and a kildee butt", "Not Broke but bent like Hell", and "plain as a river slug".

Lindsey Smith: "I will snatch you bald-headed if you do not stop that!"

Amy Hall Sorrell: "Well, I'll be a monkey's uncle."

Johnny Sowell: "You people ain't right.", "Prissy pot.", "Repent!"

Jen Spaulding: "So gooood it'd make ya slap yo moma!", "I got it at the gettin' place." and "I heard that."

Deanna Kimberlin Speight: "Fixin' too" and "Humm there King Fish!"

Kevin Spencer: "He was sharper than Dick was when Hattie died." and "He was casket sharp."

Holly Crim Springer: My mom use to fuss at us if we tried to eat at the counter saying, "Cows eat standing up."

Prisscilla Redwine Stanford: "WELL I SWANNY!"

Marcia-John Stark: I'm gonna stripe 'em legs.

Christi Weaver Stavely: "Tickled pink!", "Handy as a pocket in a shirt!" and " I reckon!"

Donna Norris Stephens: "It's hotter than a nanny goat in a pepper patch pickin' two rows at a time"

Martha Todd Stephens: "YOUINS!! GET IN HERE, ITS GONNA RAIN!"

Angela Burroughs Stewart: My Daddy always said, "Honey hush!" when somebody was lookin' good!

Rachel Morton Stewart: "Catty-whampus" (out of alignment)

Dalton Stewart: "Over yonder."

Linda Stewart: "Go bring me a switch."

David Stokes: If you walked in my Grandma Dukes home and did not speak to everyone she would say, "speak ass, mouth won't."

Christy Stout: "It's gonna take you a month of Sundays to see the light of day!!

Jenny F Strother: "Lord willing and the creek don't rise."

Amy Suiter: "My dogs are barking"

Laura Whitby Sullivan: "So good it'll make you slap your mama!"

Rusty 'Sully' Sullivan: "This food is so good you'll slap yo momma."

Tim Sullivan: "I'll knock you naked and hide your clothes!"

June Passer Sultan: "You could break an anvil with a rubber hammer." and "Just a hop skip and a jump."

Wade Hampton Sutherland: "She was batting her eyes like a frog in a hail storm."

Cecil Sutton: "Fixin to."

Linda Walker Switzer: "Ham bone knot head bone head."

Joyce Jo Gann Tankersley: 'Where's mom?..she's "nussin" the baby!!"

Beth Stobaugh Taylor: "I'll give it a lick and a promise" when she was going to iron something.

Barbara Taylor: "Your eyes are going to get stuck like that."

Bill Taylor: "Bless your little pea pickin heart."

Kreig Taylor: "Ain't that a bird dog." and "That is something else."

Linda Taylor: "You better quit crying or I'll give you something to cry about." and "Well I swanee!"

Gaius Tew: "I'm ready as a rain coat!", "I'm ready, If I

don't get to go." , "Shucking's!"

Ann Coleman Thames: "Well let me get on about my rat killin'"

Jeannie Elizabeth Casey Thomas: "Fat as a killin' hog."

Lucie May Thompson: "She has a face that has worn out a 1,000 bodies."

Phil Tillman: "If I tell you a rooster can pull a plow -hook it up."

Della Tingume: "Bless your heart honey"

Melanie Partaine Tollison: "Sweet tea grits and gossip."

Lillian High Trotter: "Any soft drink is a "coke" no matter the brand."

Mary Tubbs: mother would tell what she was cooking and then say, "and let that be it!" I find that I say that very often now.

Rachael Cheryl Hicks Tuhy: "Ain't seen you in a month of Sundays."

Sabrina Turner: "I brought you into this world and I will take you out."

Patricia Franklin Tutor: my mom used to say to the three of us, "When two are laughing and one is crying it isn't fun.”

Pam Jeffers Upchurch: “As useless as tits on a boar hog.”

Betty Jo Vail: ”That is useless as tits on a boar hog!”

Laurie Coopwood Valenzuela: “Heavens to Betsey!!!!” I still say it!!

Debbi Annaratone Vanlandingham: “Has a cat got a climbin gear?!!”

Barbara Smith Vaughan: “Where's your momma and nimm?”

Marie Anderson Vaughn: mother said “ I am so broke I can’t buy a flea on a Motorcycle Jacket”.

Sandy Verleysen: “I'm Fixin to.”

Michael Vesey: “ I was so happy I, was grinnin' like a possum eatin' yellow jackets.”

Jessica Waggoner: “Well I swunny.”

Cindy Wagner: “I got everything in this purse but a cow and a calf and I think I just heard a moo.”

Marty Walden: “What is for supper? Poke n grits. ···poke your feet under the table n grit your teeth.”

Patsy Dinkins Walker: “It's just right down the road.”

R Mike Walker: “It's soooooo good it'll make your tongue

slap your brain!", "Like a dog in high weeds!" and "Well bless his buttons!"

Dan Walker: "I'll slap the taste out of your mouth, then give ya 5 seconds to fix your face."

David Walker: Ending every sentence with the question, "Doncha know?"

Johnna Wallace: Momma said, "You have a case of the 'can't help its' or the 'don't want to's."

Melody Waller: "It's a cotton cruncher rain."

Kay Wallis: "Don't tump that over."

Lynnie Heaton: "I'm so poor I couldn't jump over a nickel to save a dime."

Joe D Walton: "TV Hopper". (When an absolute is said on TV, the opposite would happen.)

Robert RL Pete Ward: "Ward I'll stomp a mud hole in your butt and walk it dry."

Kay Culpepper Ward: When you not only don't know something but you don't want to know about that something you say "I can't know."

Debbie Parker Ware: "Access road", " I don't know whether to s**t or wind my watch", "Directly."

Murrey Malmo Watkins: "Enough to feed the second army."

Martha Watkins: My daddy said things were "bass ackards". I think he said it that way do he wouldn't have to say ass backwards.

Glenda Frederick Welch: "Come here and let me whoop you!"

Jo Teri Well: "Bless your heart!"

Angila Pittman Wells: "I am gonna knock your teeth down your throat!"

Tiffany Faith West: "He's a trip and a half."

Brenda Westbrook: My mom used to say, "Meaner than Cootie Brown," and "uglier than homemade sin."

Randy White: "Quiet as a mouse pissing on cotton!"

Carolyn Lindsey Williams: "Crazy as a sprayed roach"····favorite Southern word···"fixin."

Debi McMullen Williams: "Don't make a mountain out of a molehill!"

Suzanne Womack Williams: "Dad gum" ,"Awe shoot."

Michelle Moore Williamson: "Don't you look at me in that tone of voice." and "You are never too poor to be clean."

Sheila Rast Wilson: "I love you like a bushel & a peck & a

hug around your neck·"

Theresa O'Bryan Wilson: "You look like Ned in the Primer·"

George Tennessee Wiseman: "Quicker than Grant took Richmond·"

Marlene Safferstone Wlodawski: "Nuttier than a fruitcake·" and "Clumsy as a bull in a china shop·"

Jim Woodrick: "Drunk as Cooter Brown"

Crandall Woodson: "Don't worry 'bout the mule, just load the wagon!"

Debbie Lester Wright: "Nim"· Meaning John & Nim will be along shortly· Nim means the rest of them·

Audrey Wright: "Still kickin but not high, still floppin but caint fly·" (not doing too bad but not today good either)

Susan Thaxton Wyatt: "Madder than a four-balled tom cat!"

Any my favorite?: "Puddin' tain - ask me again and I'll tell you the same·" (I still say it!)

ABOUT THE AUTHOR

Tim Heaton grew up in Southaven, Mississippi and is a graduate of Ole Miss. After school he left the South for a career on Wall Street, and has also lived in Atlanta, Chicago, Santa Monica, Baltimore, and London, England. Tim is the proud father of Dr. Allison Pace, and two teenaged sons who reside with him and his wife Linda in Morristown, NJ. His weekly column on the proper use of Southern sayings, and other observations can be enjoyed at the online magazine: HottyToddy.com

Made in the USA
Charleston, SC
16 February 2015